CULTURAL CONNECTIONS

by
Judy Shull-Hiebenthal

illustrated by Dianne Ellis

FS-10150 Cultural Connections

FS–10150 Cultural Connections
All rights reserved–Printed in the U.S.A.
Copyright © 1994 Frank Schaffer Publications, Inc.
23740 Hawthorne Blvd.
Torrance, CA 90505

Table of Contents

Introduction

The National Council for Social Studies task force on ethnic studies states three major reasons why multicultural education is a necessity today. "1) ethnic pluralism is a growing societal reality that influences the lives of young people; 2) in one way or another, individuals acquire knowledge or beliefs, sometimes invalid, about ethnic and cultural groups; and 3) beliefs and knowledge about ethnic and cultural groups limit the perspectives of many and make a difference, often a negative difference in the opportunities and options available to members of ethnic and cultural groups. Because ethnicity, race, and class are important in the lives of many citizens of the United States, it is essential that all members of our society develop multicultural literacy, that is, a solidly based understanding of racial, ethnic, and cultural groups and their significance in U.S. society and throughout the world. Schools cannot afford to ignore their responsibility to contribute to the development of multicultural literacy and understanding. Only a well-conceived, sensitive, thorough, and continuous program of multicultural education can create the broadly based multicultural literacy so necessary for the future of our nation and world."

The purpose of this collection of materials is to provide creative ventures in multicultural studies that supplement usual classroom textbooks. *Cultural Connections* seeks to enable teachers to modify and extend existing courses of study. By using a greater variety of teaching and learning styles and establishing a setting that encourages acceptance and respect for cultural diversity, teachers AND students can move in the direction of greater understanding of and tolerance for the world's peoples.

Every cultural group reflects its value and belief systems, those patterns and ideals that give it identity. As students recognize the contributions all groups make to the character of the nation as a whole students should be able to understand and appreciate their own family heritages. Increased self-image and self-identity can serve as the base for a commitment to furthering the dignity of humankind.

The NCSS urges that students have ready access to a great variety of materials including art, history, literature, music, folklore, and views of life. These materials must permeate the total school environment and include accurate information on the diverse aspects of the histories and cultures of various racial, ethnic, and cultural groups. While multicultural education will mean different things to various disciplines, activities should be a part of all subject areas in the dimensions of content, knowledge processing, and equity. A multicultural curriculum should support diversity in language, as well, recognizing that all languages are valid forms of communication.

NCSS also adds that multicultural education must consistently address the development of the entire geocultural U.S. and the flow of cultures into the country must be viewed multi-directionally.

It is hoped that the elements of culture on the following pages will further define areas which teachers and students may wish to investigate, and that the information and activities in this publication will facilitate those dimensions of equity, content, and knowledge processing.

JUDY SHULL-HIEBENTHAL

CHAPTER 1
ARCHITECTURE

"Buildings that survive from the past are fossils of civilization. For certain early cultures that left no written records, or whose records have not been deciphered, monumental remains are the principal sources of information."
Henry-Russell Hitchcock

Of all the world's treasures, architecture is the most accessible and enduring record of culture. There are people who overlook churches, landmarks, monuments, and similar structures as a way of learning about the creative contributions of the world's peoples. Awareness and study leading to understanding adds enjoyment and appreciation of architectural examples as elements of culture.

Buildings originated as practical, useful structures. To be JUST beautiful to see was not acceptable or practical. Buildings of early eras were needed for shelters from the elements and protection from wild beasts. These ordinary, utilitarian structures rarely lasted more than a century or so, never long enough to become rare or prizes.

The sheer numbers of buildings, the profusion of architectural examples, add to the fact that people do not "see" them. To know architectural examples it is necessary to look, inquire, discover. We must ask about materials, workmanship, and purpose of the structure being studied. We must look for decorative details. We can enhance our aesthetic appreciation of architectural samples with close-up study. Proportion and line should be noted. It may help to consider architecture as three-dimensional sculpture to be viewed from all sides, several times, even at different times of day. Then we must ask, "Do I like what I see?" To know a culture's architecture is to see the signature of that culture.

1

The church of St. Basil the Blessed was built in Moscow during the reign of Ivan the Terrible. Ivan Vasilievich lived from 1530 until 1584. He served as Russia's first czar from 1547 until his death. He wished to commemorate the defeat of the Tatars. (Also spelled Tartar. They were Mongolian peoples led by Genghis Khan who overran central and western Asia as well as Eastern Europe in the thirteenth century.) Built during the span of years from 1554-1560, St. Basil's style is Byzantine, a type that evolved in Constantinople in the fifth century. Common characteristics of Byzantine style include round arches and domes.

St. Basil's domes are typically Russian and give an air of Eastern splendor. The eight onion tops honor saints on whose days Ivan the Terrible won battles against Genghis Khan's troops. Under the eight domes are chapels which surround a central sanctuary. Thus a combination of nine churches is produced.

S. Basil, Moscow

A.D. 1554 – 1560

From above, the domes form an eight-pointed star. The steeples and cupolas are decoratively carved and are of varying colors and heights. Although based on the native wooden architecture of the traditional Russian church, the extravagantly ornate domes are actually made of stone. St. Basil's church today is part of the State Historical Museum.

CONNECT 1: After looking at several views of St. Basil's church, ask eight students or eight pairs or small committees to transfer the designs from the domes to sheets of 12" x 18" construction paper. Have them use paints or chalks in bright colors to reproduce the varying designs.

CONNECT 2: St. Basil's is near Red Square and the Kremlin. Ask interested students to prepare a map that could be used by a visitor to Moscow and set up a walking tour that would enable the visitor to see all the famous spots within walking distance of St. Basil's.

Located on the dusty plains of Agra, 125 miles southeast of Delhi, India, the Taj Mahal is known as one of the world's most beautiful buildings. The "Crown of Palaces" has been called the seventh wonder of the modern world and man's greatest tribute to woman. It is India's greatest tourist attraction.

The Taj Mahal was commissioned by Shah Jahan, a Mogul emperor, for his wife, Mumtaz, who died giving birth to their fourteenth child. In architecture the graceful Mogul style resulted when Persian and Hindu traditions were combined. The symmetrical style of the Taj is derived from the gateway of an Indian mosque.

The entrance level chamber has false tombs of Mumtaz and Shah Jahan. They are actually buried in duplicate tombs at the lower level. Mumtaz's sarcophagus is decorated with patterns of calligraphy and floral motifs of roses, poppies, and other flowers. Within the Taj are carved inlaid marble screens set at the top of the walls. Geometric Persian designs cover the surfaces of all floors.

Approximately 22,000 laborers and craftsman worked 24 hours a day for 22 years building the Taj Mahal. An architect from Lahore drew the plans and, according to an inscription on the structure, it was built by a Turk. Calligraphy work was done by a person known as Shirazi. It was finished in 659 A.D. The emperor beggared his empire in the building of the tomb for his favorite wife.

The Taj is actually a red brick building encased in white marble (symbol of purity of love). Its four sides resemble towering arches set in rectangular surfaces. They resemble doors to Persian mosques and are flanked by tall octagonal structures with arched balconies. The huge, bulbous dome crown is raised on a drum in the central area. Four large circular minarets crowned with canopies stand freely at the corners.

It is interesting to note that the dome atop this beautiful building is remarkably similar in shape and texture to stacks of hay found in the farmland in the countryside near Agra.

From a distance the exterior appears plain. Closeup, inlaid, semiprecious gems and stones (35 types) are visible including agates, garnets, and jade.

As impressive as the building itself are the grounds. A long, rectangular pool of water reflects the trees and the Persian walled gardens that surround the Taj. Formally landscaped, symmetrical gardens contain cypress trees and flower beds. Again the white marble is in striking contrast to the red sandstone of the other buildings on the grounds.

Shah Jahan had planned a second Taj of black marble, a mirror image, to be his tomb. But that was not accomplished and he lies beside Mumtaz on the lower level of the structure.

The Taj Mahal is one of the most photographed buildings in the world. A bit of a chameleon, the Taj is said to be rosy pink at dusk and dawn, to give off a bright glare during the day, and a phosphorescent glow in the darkness of night. Even the pollution of the modern world has done little to diminish the majesty of this marvelous example of architecture.

CONNECT 1: Locate several copies of pictures of the Taj Mahal for students to study. Ask them to point out examples of symmetry. "Divide" the Taj into parts that could be reproduced with symmetry—for instance, each minaret, the central dome, the front view, the reflection in the pool in the front. Challenge the group to reproduce as nearly as possible the entire structure by using symmetrical shapes drawn, then cut.

Ask students to search for objects or parts of your classroom that offer examples of symmetry. Have them create other designs using symmetry.

CONNECT 2: Take a walking tour of the neighborhood of your school, or select a business district which may offer a variety of architectural styles. Ask students to point out symmetrical or asymmetrical features. If possible, secure local histories to learn the construction stories of older buildings. Ask students to reproduce a building or structure in a format of their choice.

CONNECT 3: From illustrations, from the text, or from reference books in the library, ask students to study the geometric designs that are a prominent part of Persian artistic style. Have them use the idea of tessellations to create one single pattern, reproduce it many times to fill a 6" x 8" sheet of paper, and add color or shading for contrast.

THE ALHAMBRA

The building of the Alhambra began in 1230 on a hill overlooking Granada, Spain. It was a fortified palace for Moorish kings of the Nosrid dynasty. The Alhambra's name is derived from the Arabic phrase *Kalatalhamra,* meaning "red castle." It is the most famous of classical works of Moslem architecture in Spain. Some say it is the best in all of Europe.

The tall rock hill with steep cliffs on which the palace was constructed provided natural protection from enemies. The light, mud brick inner walls were faced with burnt-red brick. The fortress with square towers, severe walls, and a wooden roof belies the beauty within.

Inside, everything is light, cool, and airy. The floors are of polished marble, walls are richly decorated with colorful designs in stone, and there are many narrow keyhole-shaped windows. Ceilings are of white plaster skillfully carved with patterns and figures. Glazed tiles and plaster ornaments add further to the sumptuous design. Enclosed courts feature statuary and fountains. The Moorish kings who spent the summers in the heat of Spain surrounded themselves with water, shooting skyward from fountains or lying still in pools encircled with plants and flowers.

The arcades (series of arches supported by columns or pillars) have several arch patterns—horseshoe, high and slightly pointed round arch, and the flat pointed arch that is almost triangular. All buildings are adorned with thousands of arabesques, complex, ornate designs of intertwined flowers, plants, and geometric figures.

The Court of Lions is probably the most famous portion of the Alhambra. Arcades can be seen on all four sides. A cloister (enclosed walkway) is featured running along the inside of the colonnade. A huge marble basin with 12 lions is located in the center. An interesting sidelight to this statuary is that the Moors who were Moslems were not supposed to carve statues of living things. It is believed that perhaps the creatures are Christian lions carved elsewhere and "imported" to the Alhambra.

The Alhambra has been extensively restored to preserve the artistic contribution made by the Moors. Their belief that one should value beauty and choose to live surrounded by it is evident in this structure.

The story is told that a blind beggar approached a Spanish nobleman and his lady to ask for coins. The nobleman turned to his companion and said, "Give money, my lady, for surely in life there is no suffering so great, as being blind in Granada."

CONNECT 1: Point out special architectural vocabulary seen in this story. Adding a few other chosen terms, new or familiar, ask students to create a crossword puzzle with detailed clues. Sharing and completing the puzzle with others in the class should result in all students learning spelling and vocabulary words unique to architecture.

CONNECT 2: Supply students with an outline map of Spain. Direct them to locate famous places on that map. Include a brief caption-like description of the site. They may choose 10-12 places or you may suggest these:

Granada - location of Alhambra
Madrid - capital and location of Gaudi's coke bottle church
Toledo - subject of El Greco's *View of Toledo*
Seville - known for bullfights among other things
Homes of Spanish artists Velasquez and Picasso
Any other places pertinent to your study

THE EIFFEL TOWER

Gustave Eiffel was born in Dijon, France, in 1832. He was a brilliant chemist turned structural engineer who pioneered techniques for bridge design during the Age of Iron.

Among Eiffel's accomplishments are the Douro River bridge in Portugal, the movable observatory dome in Nice, France, and the masterful bridge in the south of France, the Garabit railroad bridge. The Garabit structure was 1,667 feet long with one single spanning arch of 544 feet. Ten years after finishing the Garabit bridge, Frédéric Auguste Bartholdi sought out Eiffel to assist him with his project, a gift to the American people from the people of France. The versatile French engineer devised the iron skeleton for Bartholdi's Statue of Liberty. Liberty's basic construction became the formula used in building modern skyscrapers.

In 1889, Eiffel designed a structure for the Paris Exhibition. The Eiffel Tower contains 7,000 short tons (6,400 metric tons) of iron and steel. The huge wrought iron skeleton of the tower rises 984 feet (300 m) from its 330-foot (101 m) square base on the Champ de Mars in Paris.

The tower is formed by four immense pylons that meet at the top. The arches one sees when studying the tower are merely decorative links. (This idea of ornamentation over solid construction became popular later in the Art Nouveau era.) Elevators and stairways lead to the top. There are restaurants, weather data gathering stations, and places set aside for experiments of various kinds. During World War I, the tower was an information gathering station. And since 1953 it has been used to transmit television signals.

Its total cost in 1889 was $1 million. Although it was meant to be a temporary part of the Paris skyline, it remains there today.

Metal structures like Gustave Eiffel's tower actually are not very durable compared to stone and timber architecture. It is only through constant maintenance that the Eiffel Tower survives.

At the time of its construction, many Parisians considered Gustave Eiffel's tower to be a dishonor and a disgrace to their city. Now his poetic combination of math, art, and technology symbolizes the "City of Lights."

CONNECT 1: Divide the class into two research groups, one to gather information about the Eiffel Tower, the second to look for details about the Statue of Liberty. Have students use drawings and pictures to create a display that compares and contrasts these two famous structures. Individuals within the groups could be assigned specific research tasks such as actual size, materials used, and time spent in construction. Data gathered could be charted to provide a quick visual comparison.

Further avenues of investigation might include local structures that share similar construction features, local engineers or builders who could speak to the class, local history texts describing bridge construction.

CONNECT 2: Students who may find bridge construction of interest to them could investigate various bridge styles. These could be shared via pencil drawings or water color paintings (include names and labels), built with toothpicks, straws, or ice cream sticks, or made of heavier materials. More substantial models could be tested with weights to determine different strengths of different styles.

Since the Stone Age, Scandinavia has had its own art tradition. Certain "enrichments" were gathered from cultural centers in southern Europe through the years. One clear difference that can be seen between northern and southern European art is the predominance of decorative design among Scandinavians rather than representations of the human figure. Also the prevalence of wood rather than the use of clay, metal, or stone and particularly the use of wood for architecture is more highly developed in Scandinavia than in other parts of Europe.

Viking ships are one example of this. Their carved sterns of dragons' tails and bows of heads of dragons, as well as intricately carved friezes of animals on oak planks, reflect exceptional artistic achievement.

During the eleventh and twelfth centuries there occurred an artistic blending of Scandinavian pagan traditions and Christian art. The result was the picturesque wooden stave church, an architectural form native to Scandinavian peoples. Similar wooden structures were also built in Eastern Europe beginning in the late Middle Ages. During the twelfth century hundreds of the Scandinavian variety were constructed. Only 32 of more than 800 are preserved today in Norway.

The stave church's sophisticated framework was placed on a foundation of stone. This aided in the church's longevity. Four corner posts called staves (from *hiornst-fir*) rose from four horizontal beams (*chassis sills*). These formed the basic framework. Upright beams supported the masts. Thus a series of open aisles were formed around the center or nave. The sanctuary or altar was a small shed projecting from one end of the nave. Upright planks formed the outer walls. There were often four or more ranks of masts that supported an equal number of triangular frames diminishing in size at the top of the building.

The interior of most of the stave churches was decorated with Viking and Christian motifs. Reaching from the peaks of the gabled roofs were dragon-headed ornaments.

As congregations became too large for the stave churches more traditional stone structures replaced them. Sometimes regarded as folk art, stave churches are all but ignored by more formal architectural writers.

CONNECT 1: Ask students to secure a copy of *Stateman's Yearbook* from the library. This book will have addresses for embassies or ambassadors from Scandinavian countries. Students should write a proper business letter requesting information about this unique architectural example and share the material that they receive with the class.

CONNECT 2: Students may wish to read and/or research the Viking chapter of Scandinavian history. Models of the Viking ships or villages could be constructed. Cooperative learning groups may also wish to use the paper person pattern described in this book to create families of Vikings to display in the Viking village.

Direct class members to samples of Viking literature including the stories of Leif Ericson and Eric the Red.

CONNECT 3: This might also be an appropriate time to compare and contrast stave churches with the architectural style of churches in your own neighborhoods, communities, or cities. A photographic walking trip or a riding tour could be arranged so that students could take pictures of local church styles. Back in the room, photographs could be studied and compared to those of Scandinavian stave churches, and drawings could be made of those local buildings students feel most closely resemble those of northern Europe.

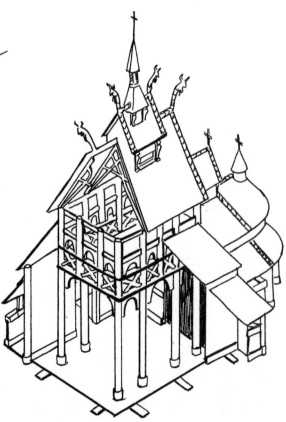

Of the 900 stone circles known today all across the British Isles, Stonehenge is the most famous Neolithic monument. It was built and rebuilt by early Bretons who used the site as a location for a center of community. It is fairly certain that Stonehenge, the open air structure, was used to study the sun and the moon. It may have been a place to recognize and celebrate events in the heavens. Or it may have been used to predict astronomical phenomena.

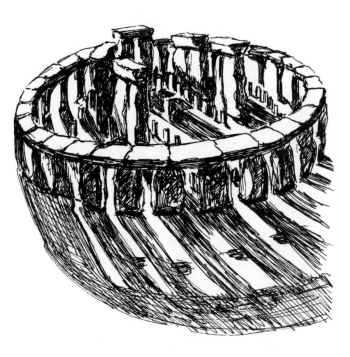

The construction of Stonehenge spanned 40 generations and 1,000 years and was completed in three stages. In its first stage, Stonehenge had an earthen circle 97.5 m (320 feet) in diameter. No doubt it was created by placing a wooden peg at the circle's center. Attached to the peg was an oxhide rope with sharp object tied at the end which marked the circumference. Two embankments were separated by a ditch dug through the chalky earth. Sticks, antler picks, and shovels made from oxen's shoulder bones were tools available for accomplishing this task. A tall pillar of gray sandstone (sarsen) from nearby Marlborough was erected at the only break in the circle. It was named the Heel Stone. About 2100 B.C., 56 holes were added along the circumference. They are now known as Aubrey Holes, named after John Aubrey who discovered them in the 1630s. Excavations revealed bits of human bones and evidence of fire.

The Beaker peoples from Holland and the Rhineland remodeled Stonehenge 500 years later. Because they were widely traveled and were familiar with the blue stones from Prescelly Mountains in Wales, they selected and transported 80 blue stones weighing four tons each. This becomes a remarkable feat when you consider that the shortest route from Wales to the Salisbury Plains is 300 miles. The blue stones were positioned to form a double circle in the middle of the circle at Stonehenge known as "The Avenue." It is fairly certain that they never completed their project because there were stones dragged to the entrance which were never used and the circle had an open gap in it.

About 1600 B.C. the second stage of building began. The unfinished circle of blue stones was dismantled by the inhabitants of Wessec. The blue stones were replaced with 80 sarsen stone blocks. Sarsen was a natural sandstone gathered from nearby Marlborough Downs. They were probably brought to the site via a movable track of oak rollers. Inside the chalk circle the sarsen stones were tilted in a ring of pits dug to hold their bases. Then they were straightened and stabilized. Curved *lintels* (horizontal top pieces) were added over each pair of uprights. This produced an inner horseshoe of *trilithons* (tri = three; lith = stone; trilithons = 3 stones). The sarsen stones in the center weighed about 25 tons each. The lintels were close to 7 tons apiece. The lintels were cut and fitted together using the mortise and tenon method. All in all this must be considered a stupendous accomplishment.

The final stage of reconstruction occurred when the uprights of the oval structure were reset into the horseshoe we see today. There may have been 60 blue stones originally set rather closely together but they have long since disappeared.

Stonehenge has suffered much through the centuries. Stones were broken up to be used for local building projects, for repairing roads, and for people who wished to have souvenirs. In 1922 the British government began to restore Stonehenge. Some of the scattered stones were returned to the structure. It is carefully protected today.

CONNECT 1: Ask students to draw humorous cartoons that offer a rather non-sensical explanation of how Stonehenge may have been constructed. Display the cartoons on a bulletin board for all to see.

CONNECT 2: Ask students to gather or create a set of rectangular wooden blocks that could be used to demonstrate the construction stages of Stonehenge. (This is an excellent example of the need for students to work together cooperatively.) Then have them make paper tags to explain the unique Stonehenge vocabulary...*lintel, mortise, tenon, lith,* and *trilithon.*

CONNECT 3: Discuss with students the policies that governments must develop to preserve and protect monuments like Stonehenge. Assign students to prepare a warning sign (concise but complete) to place at the approach to Stonehenge informing visitors of the rules and regulations for its use and enjoyment.

Have students consider the following questions. Are there places in your own community it might be necessary to protect? Could a student action committee take on such a project? Through which political or governmental channels is it necessary to go to achieve such a goal?

"Pure invention is rare in architecture, and originality more commonly manifests itself in the purposeful adjustment of traditional forms. The Romans were selective in their borrowings and adapted everything to new specifications."

Spiro Kostof

And so the Roman Colosseum (from the Latin *colosseus* meaning "huge") consists of two Greek theaters removed from the hillside to the center of town and placed end to end. The Colosseum's construction was begun in the seventies A.D. by the Flavian emperors who followed the downfall of Nero. Vespasian began the work and the emperor Domitian completed the project in A.D. 82.

The Roman Colosseum was built over an artificial lake that was on the grounds of a rambling palace that had been destroyed by fire in A.D. 64. The awe-inspiring ellipse measuring 620' x 513' was used for entertainment events popular with Romans in the first century, including beast fights, combat among gladiators, and mock sea battles. The Colosseum was designed to hold 45,000 to 50,000 spectators. It is four stories high, the three lowest being arch-bearing piers. Its arcades (lines or arches supported on piers or columns) influenced Renaissance builders. The arena itself was 180' x 187' and was surrounded by a wall 15' in height. There were 80 external openings on each story which facilitated movement of the crowds in a matter of minutes.

The foundation of the Colosseum is lava. The walls are brick and tufa (a building material of porous, gray, volcanic stone). Pumice stone was used for the vaults or arches. The exterior facade, a blend of solid grandeur and grace, was constructed from a limestone block known as travertine. The columns and seats were made of marble.

More evidence of borrowed ideas can be seen in the external columns that adorn the Colosseum. Greek, Doric, Ionian, and Corinthian columns are stacked to produce a decorative touch to the exterior.

CONNECT 1: Have students design posters advertising an upcoming event at the Colosseum in Rome. They could use an illustration of the building as it appeared in Roman times as the background and give pertinent facts about the entertainment. They should include information about the participants, date, time, and decide if the spectators must pay (in Roman coins, of course). Display finished entertainment posters in the classroom.

CONNECT 2: Ask each student to write a letter to the editor of the local Roman paper, expressing his/her concern that the contests at the Colosseum involving animals are inhumane. Specific examples should illustrate the point. Then each student should ask two friends to write replies to the letter. One of these letters will agree and the second will disagree.

CONNECT 3: Students should investigate recent photos of the Colosseum and note the traffic pattern in and around the areas of the Colosseum. Ask them to draw conclusions about heavy traffic and the deterioration of the ancient structure and offer suggestions for alternate routes or other solutions.

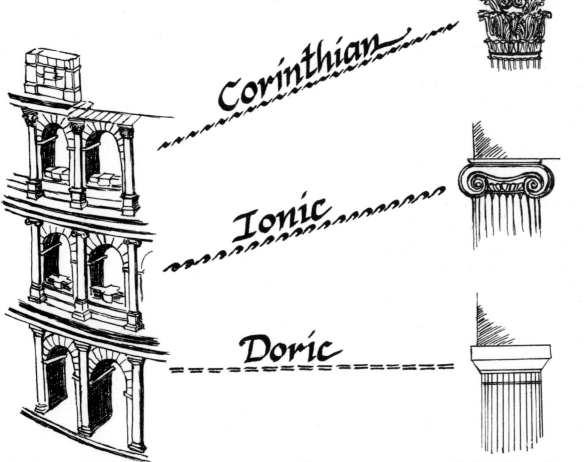

Corinthian

Ionic

Doric

The most primitive form of housing was caves. In some parts of the world, namely Italy, Spain, Turkey, and Tunisia, whole villages of people resided in underground caves or mountain caves. These people were known as *troglodytes.*

Nearly every natural material available to man has been used for construction of homes. Cabins of logs were built in forested areas and stone structures with thatched roofs have been constructed in places with few trees. Nomadic peoples such as the Lapps, the Bedouins, or peoples of Africa used animal skins and lightweight reeds to build their homes. These materials were easily disposed of when it came time to move on.

Thick stone-walled homes placed close together or actually attached were whitewashed to reflect heat and contribute to comfortable coolness in hot climates. In cold parts of the world buildings were placed close and around a courtyard for added protection for humans and their animals.

Today's metropolitan areas feature high-rise apartments and condominiums that facilitate busy life styles and an increased older, retired population. Yet many common features from the past are seen in these present- day structures.

Here are some interesting glimpses of traditional styles of building, some unique examples of regional cultures.

SWITZERLAND - Alpine chalets made of warm long-lasting wood feature overhanging roofs that retain thick blankets of snow for added insulation in winter. Burghers' houses had designs called *sgraffiti* scratched into the plaster, then finished with bright colors.

GREECE - High roofs were needed for proper ventilation in the hot climate of the Greek islands. The barrel vault was the simple solution for comfortable temperatures. In addition this style made excellent use of the ready supply of stone.

FRANCE - Traditional homes of the Bretons on the northwest coast of France included shelter for man and beast under one roof. Medieval era buildings in Strasbourg have carved wooden balconies that lean toward the street, high-pitched roofs, and dormer windows.

HOLLAND - Bricks once exported from England were used to build the foundations of traditional Dutch farmhouses. The German half-frame or half-timber style was often used. In large cities Dutch houses were tall and narrow. Decorative gables beautified these homes that made the most of precious soil. Earth was limited, but air was free!

SWEDEN - A version of the Scandinavian log house was later copied by people who settled in New England. It was designed so that the joints tightened as the weight of the house pressed downward. In time the structure became more insulated and watertight.

IRELAND - Thatched roofs were common on the stone buildings found in this part of the world. Reeds were cheap, durable, and provided good insulation. Those advantages were balanced with the disadvantage of the increased risk of fire.

SPAIN - Thick stone walls of homes on the Mediterranean were white-washed and stuccoed to provide insulation from the heat of the sun. In neighboring Portugal, well-to-do, land-owning families had their family crests carved into an outer wall of their rather plain homes made of granite.

ENGLAND - Country homes in the British Isles were typically built of red brick. In areas where chalk was plentiful, flint was a commonly used material.

MOROCCO - Berber village homes had thatched roofs with a "shelf" of over-hanging mud to provide good drainage during the rainstorms. The sun-dried mud hardened well, creating a substantial building material.

TUNISIA - Barrel-vaulted stone homes, called *ghorfas*, were built by former cave dwellers who were forced from the mountains of northern Africa. They moved to valley areas where they found more accessible supplies of food and water.

ICELAND - Farmhouses were traditionally built into the hillsides to conserve heat. Turf roofs were used by animals for grazing. This roof style was transferred to buildings in the cities as well. Steeper angles of roofs and close proximity to neighboring buildings were two adaptations from rural to urban areas.

CHINA - In the Orient, private homes with walled enclosures were common in rural areas. Urban homes also had inner courtyards. Both were simple in structure and appearance. The Chinese garden was inseparable from the home.

Mongolian tents featured a system of underground heating. Tibetan villagers constructed their community villages on terraced hillsides.

JAPAN - Japanese architecture has always been considered a communion with the environment. Freedom of space was created with sliding walls, verandas, translucent screens, and tatami mats based on the modular system. Building materials were exploited to establish harmony with nature.

AFRICA - Traditional African homes were separate buildings that together made up a homestead. This collection of structures was usually surrounded by a wall or fence. They varied immensely across the continent.

Zulu peoples in the southeastern tip of Africa had homes symmetrically arranged in two concentric stockades. The inside circle kept cattle. Storage pits were often dug beneath this smaller circle. The chief and each wife had a "room." Additional buildings were used for unmarried sons and for grain storage.

Nuba people's homesteads were built in a ring-shaped pattern. Individual buildings were linked by walls or fences. The walls of the buildings were made of red clay with gravel mixed in. The "homes" included bedrooms, quarters for the pigs and goats, and grinding and store rooms.

Yoruba villagers lived in towns in the forested areas of western Nigeria. Houses here were built around one large courtyard and around tiny 1 m diameter areas used to allow light into the homes. This tiny yard also served to catch precious rain water. The outside walls were built of puddled mud. In urban areas the plan was much the same except that an additional room was created for craftwork.

Somolo people lived in the southern part of Upper Volta. They built multistory homes with walls of puddled mud. Ceilings and roofs consisted of support posts covered with palm fronds. There were several circular buildings with a tiny courtyard for each house. There could be as many as 20 rooms for wives, children, kitchens, storage, granaries, and grinding rooms.

CONNECT 1: As you study different locations and cultures around the world, assign an individual or group to be in charge of illustrating historic and/or modern homes. Collect these drawings and put them into a reference book format. Include as much text as needed to make comparisons among the peoples you study.

A second option would be to make smaller illustrations and create an ongoing chart that would show similarities and differences.

A third option would be to ask each student to photograph or draw his/her home. Then these could be added to the chart or book as architectural styles are studied.

CONNECT 2: Students can search magazines for colored pictures of homes, present or past, and create a collage of structures.

CONNECT 3: Ask students to imagine, think, and plan what they consider to be an ideal home in which to live. Start with scale drawings on grid paper. Transfer the drawing to three-dimensional models featuring as many actual materials as possible. Display the homes for all to see.

CONNECT 4: Invite a local builder of homes to come to your classroom to discuss his/her work. Students may wish to prepare questions for the guest prior to the visit. Blueprints may be of interest to the class. Building codes and restrictions, up-to-date materials, and styles and features that are in demand could be discussed. The speaker could discuss . Preparation for this career might be shared. Ask your class to brainstorm possible topics.

CONNECT 5: Take your students on a walking tour of your school building. Look for architectural features and details that are seen everyday, but are overlooked by the casual viewer. One such example is the myriad of colors and patterns in brick. Students may be interested in the time line used to build your school. Back in the room, allow time and materials for groups or individuals who may wish to REDESIGN a trouble area, an overcrowded hall, or a room that is too small.

AFRICAN NUBA

GERMANY

21

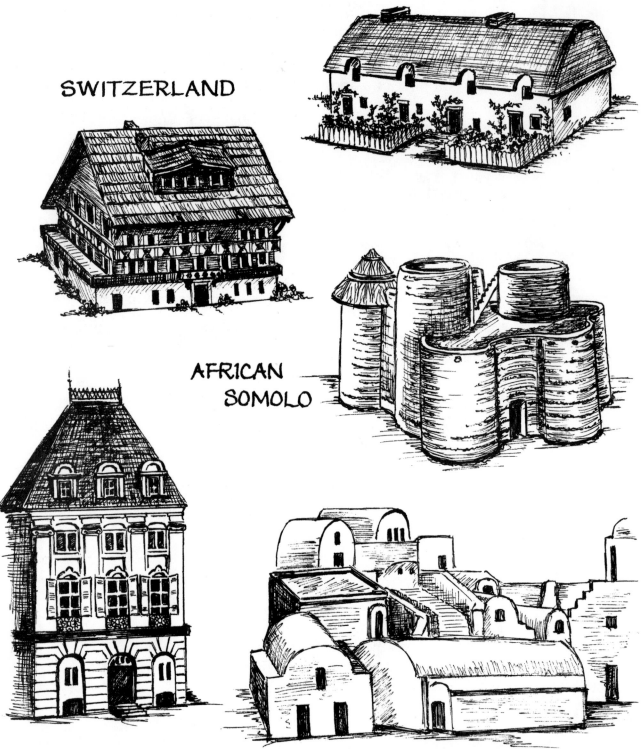

IRELAND

SWITZERLAND

AFRICAN
SOMOLO

URBAN
HOLLAND

GREECE

HIDDEN TREASURE

Unscramble each word at the top of the page. Then place it in the corresponding numbered space at the bottom of the page.

You will produce an interesting connection between an ancient architectural treasure and modern times.

1. dyoat   1. _ _ _ _ _
2. gdinse   2. _ _ _ _ _ _
3. no   3. _ _
4. mooClsesu   4. _ _ _ _ _ _ _ _ _
5. fo   5. _ _
6. dbsae   6. _ _ _ _ _ _
7. rtossp   7. _ _ _ _ _ _
8. teh   8. _ _ _
9. idssaumt   9. _ _ _ _ _ _ _ _
10. rea   10. _ _ _
11. eth   11. _ _ _

$$\underset{7}{\_\ \_\ \_\ \_\ \_\ \_}\qquad \underset{9}{\_\ \_\ \_\ \_\ \_\ \_\ \_}\qquad \underset{1}{\_\ \_\ \_\ \_}$$

$$\underset{10}{\_\ \_\ \_}\qquad \underset{6}{\_\ \_\ \_\ \_}\qquad \underset{3}{\_\ \_}\qquad \underset{11}{\_\ \_\ \_}\qquad \underset{2}{\_\ \_\ \_\ \_}$$

$$\underset{5}{\_\ \_}\qquad \underset{8}{\_\ \_\ \_}\qquad \underset{4}{\_\ \_\ \_\ \_\ \_\ \_\ \_}.$$

In this space, make a quick pencil sketch of the ancient architectural design mentioned in the puzzle.

ANALYZE ARCHITECTURE

Here are some architectural "ingredients" that are commonly found in buildings, no matter what their age. Secure permission to scout around your school to see if you can locate these features. Of course, you will need to know what you are searching for.

When you find these features, make a quick sketch and jot down the location.

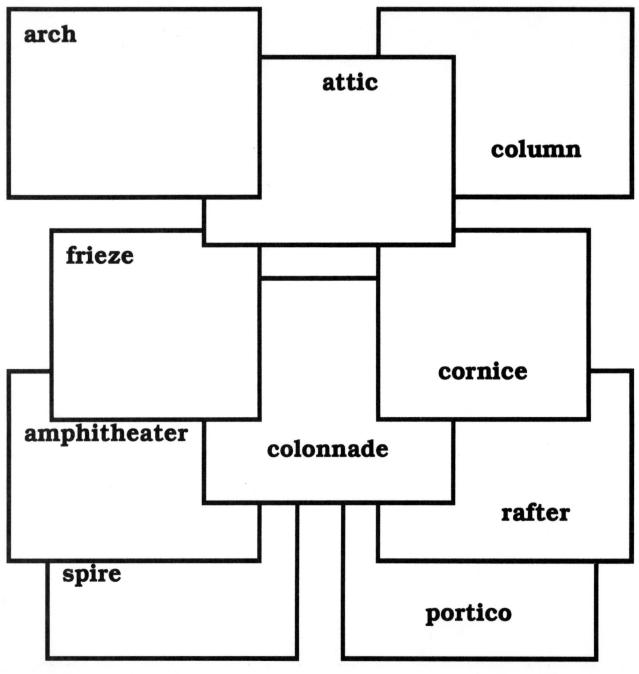

arch

attic

column

frieze

cornice

amphitheater

colonnade

rafter

spire

portico

ONE + ONE + ONE + ONE . . .

Spanish architect, Antonio Gaudi, is known for his most unusual style in architecture. Read about some of his structures to see a few examples for yourself. In La Sagrada Familia, his unfinished project in Barcelona, Spain, you can see how he took a variety of features from all types of architecture and incorporated them into the design of this church.

Follow Gaudi's lead. Take some special feature from each of the examples of architecture in this section. Draw them below as one unique structure. On the back of this page, list the features and buildings separately.

MY NEW BUILDING

WHAT/WHO AM I?

I am found in the Far East.
I am used by Hindus and Buddhists.
I have many "layers."
    What am I?

I stretch for 1,500 miles.
I was built between the years
    246 and 209 B.C.
I am wide enough that six horsemen
    can ride side by side on me.
    What am I?

I have a rectangular base.
I have four triangular sides.
I have been used for burials.
    What am I?

I was built to honor a goddess.
I am seen on the Acropolis.
I am in ruins today.
    What am I?

Can you guess the answers to these architectural riddles? Select four to six of your own architectural examples from around the world. Write clues for them. Notice the first is more difficult and vague than the rest. If you would like to make a contest of this, award three points if the building or structure is guessed on the first clue, two points for the second, etc. If you would like, award a point for a correctly spelled answer, or add a point if its general location can be pointed out on a world map after it is guessed.

LAYERS OF LIBERTY

If you watch a structure under construction, you can see its skeleton. But as the building is finished, it is easy to forget what the infrastructure looked like.

Below are the skeletal frameworks, front and side views, of the Statue of Liberty. These frameworks are the result of the genius of Gustave Eiffel.

Secure permission to make a transparency of the skeletons. Then on a second piece of transparent film, create the Statue of Liberty as we see it in the harbor. Prepare a presentation for the class in which you discuss the skeleton. Then overlay the first sheet with your finished sketch.

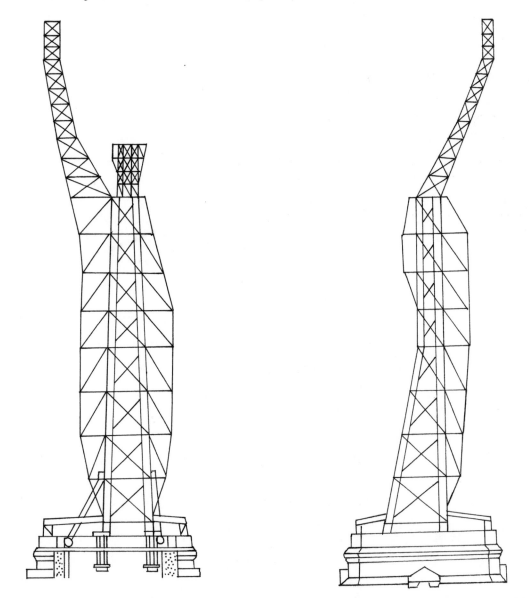

CHAPTER 2
ART AND ARTISTS

Art is the record of mankind. Its remains are older than humans' tools and homes. By the time writing appeared, art was thousands of years old, buried and forgotten in the caves of southern Europe. Humankind's first alphabet was a set of pictures—hieroglyphics created by the Egyptians. And it is with Egypt that the story of art really begins. The Egyptians' work stood for centuries as a model for the world.

Across the waters of the Mediterranean via the island of Crete, the next chapter in art history was written. The Greeks were considered by some critics to be the greatest artists of all time. Their paintings, however, did not survive. We know of their artistic progress from the records left in the numerous red and black-figure vases. Statues and Greek architecture are also an important part of that story.

The Romans learned from the Greeks. The combination of Roman and Greek styles was known as *classical art.* Roman wall paintings have survived thanks to the eruption of Mt. Vesuvius and the burying of Pompeii and Herculaneum.

During the Dark Ages less attention was paid to art. Artists showed much less skill than in preceding eras. In the Middle Ages that followed, art existed mostly for the Church within the walls of the monasteries. Native artisans of the tribal peoples of Europe made their contributions.

Religion took the back seat as Europe awoke from the sleep of the Middle Ages. People opened their eyes and minds. It was an age of new learning...the Renaissance had begun.

Painters and sculptors made exciting new discoveries. Italy became the center of the rebirth. The fever of the Renaissance soon spread to northern European cities as well. In Germany, The Netherlands, and Belgium new directions for art were opened. Portrait painting, art for display in the home, art as something to look at was being created. With the coming of the Reformation, emphasis on religious art was greatly diminished.

Spanish and French art in the fifteenth century focused on the courts of the kings and queens. Landscape painting was high on the popularity list in the seventeenth century.

The Romantic Movement took form in the late 1700s and early 1800s. Common people involved in ordinary tasks appeared on canvas, as city dwellers sought escape from their humdrum lives. Interest in remote places increased at this time. France was the center of the art world as the nineteenth century approached.

Impressionistic and Expressionistic Movements were seen at the close of the 1800s and into the early 1900s. These were interlocked and overlapped with the styles labeled abstract, cubist, and surrealistic. Artists from all around the world participated in these trends.

Art has been a mirror of the human mind, changing as it changed. This incomplete look at art history points out the relationship between cultures, the influence one has upon another, and clearly indicates there is no end to this story. Time lines and tables illustrate this most clearly. (Consult any reference book on art history for such a time line.) Such a chart will show contributions from around the globe.

Art is about looking, seeing, and drawing conclusions. The art criticism sheet included here will guide students as they study any art reproduction. Using reproductions from artists all over the world, setting the historical scene, and creating interdisciplinary links will help teachers and students grow as appreciators of art as a cultural connection.

MARC CHAGALL

Marc Chagall lived from 1887 to 1985. Vitebsk near Minsk in Russia was his home. He was the oldest of eight children, six boys and two girls. The Chagall family was close and loving. Chagall's extended family of aunts and uncles, grandma and grandpa appeared in later years in his paintings.

Chagall was considered a dreamy child, everyone's favorite. In a private school early in his life, he studied Talmud, the Jewish book of tradition and law. The Bible was also included in his studies. When he was 13, he began attending public school where drawing and geometry were his favorite subjects. Chagall also took singing and violin lessons. He learned to dance well. In his spare time he enjoyed writing poetry.

Chagall began drawing after a friend showed him ink drawings that he had made. It soon became apparent that this was what Chagall wanted to do with his life.

In 1906 Chagall began studying art in St. Petersburg. Four years later he moved to France to continue his studies. There was frequent traveling over the next 10 to 20 years...in Europe, to America, Mexico, and Israel.

Chagall's early paintings represent memories of his childhood in Russia, events, people, and everyday places. His works are colorful collages of dreams, symbols, and unusual combinations of people and places.

Marc Chagall said about his choice for a lifetime's work, "Painting was more necessary for me than food. It seemed like a window through which I could have taken flight into another world." As you study his paintings you may conclude that that was just what Chagall did.

CONNECT 1: Encourage students to secure pictures or reproductions from the school library or from the art department. An art history book will probably include reprints of Chagall's works. Have them use the art criticism sheet found at the beginning of this section to "look" at a Marc Chagall work and use a pencil to mark appropriate parts while working through the checklist.

If several reproductions are available, distribute them among cooperative-learning groups. Ask selected students to orally share their findings and opinions. Have the class compare and contrast subject matter, colors used, and other features in the available reproductions and look for familiar family members or scenes from Chagall's early life in a small Russian village.

CONNECT 2: Point out to students that Marc Chagall's paintings not only reflected his childhood memories but also tell us of the life of a Jewish family in Russia at the turn of the century. Have students locate evidence in Chagall's paintings of the uniqueness of this cultural group and look for such things as clothing, religious practices, occupations, and architectural styles. Discuss how these examples of man's art truly reflect life at a given time in history. Ask if anyone in class has viewed the movie *Fiddler on the Roof.* It, too, offers similar glances at the Russian Jews' daily living.

CONNECT 3: Students can create a time line divided by decades starting at 1880 and running through 1990. On one side they should note major happenings in the life of Chagall and on the other side key world events. Have them draw conclusions about Chagall's life as it paralleled world happenings.

CONNECT 4: Chagall wrote poetry in his spare time when he was young. After studying a favorite reproduction, ask students to write poems to the artist telling him how they feel about what he has painted. Especially interesting works to view include *Paris Through a Window, Peasant Life, Over Vitebsk, The Flying Carriage, I and the Village, Russian Wedding,* and *Green Violinist.*

CONNECT 5: Make copies of the unfinished portion of the man with the green face from Chagall's *I and the Village* which can be found in the student activity pages at the end of this chapter. Direct students to imagine what the rest of the man looks like. If interest and time permit, they can create the remainder of the body to see the entire figure of the man, finish the drawing, and add color.

Ernest Raboff wrote, "For a painter to become an artist, for a craftsman or professional to become a truly creative person, that individual must be a scientist, an objective observer, a naturalist, and a humanist." Raboff was describing German artist, Albrecht Dürer.

Dürer was born in Nuremberg, Germany, in 1471. Before the 1500s artists in northern Europe were still believed to be instruments of God, relaying religious ideas through art. In southern Europe artists were regarded as individuals and for some time they had publicly declared this status by signing their works of art. Albrecht Dürer liked that idea. You can see his familiar monogram on most of his paintings.

GERMANY

Albrecht received his early training from his goldsmith father who taught him engraving. Later he was apprenticed to the shop of Wolgemut where he learned painting and how to make woodcuts. He traveled to learn from established artists, Jan Van Eyck among them.

Albrecht Dürer was insatiably curious and a life-long learner. He painted portraits, landscapes, trees, animals, and flowers. He once wrote, "I want to know something of all things."

His detailed drawing of a rhinoceros with skin like a coat of armor was sent to the king of Portugal. His columbine and peony paintings look real enough to be photos from the garden. *Young Hare* (1502) is a masterpiece of detail with every whisker and hair visible. Reverence for nature and creation are seen in these realistic works.

Albrecht Dürer said, "That must be a strangely dull head which never trusts itself to find out anything fresh but only travels among the old path simply following others and not daring to reflect for itself."

CONNECT 1: Albrecht Dürer was one of the first painters to produce realistic scenes from nature done with watercolors. Take your students outside to a location that offers closeups of nature. Have them sketch simple things—trees, plants, weeds. Add watercolors to the drawings. Display the pictures with a reproduction of Dürer's *The Large Piece of Turf* if it is available. This might be a suitable product to be included in a portfolio.

CONNECT 2: Albrecht Dürer and Leonardo da Vinci were contemporaries. Direct students to use library resources (CD Rom, non-fiction books, vertical file) to locate sketches and paintings by these two men. Let students set up a table display with captions that point out similarities and differences in the men's works.

CONNECT 3: Ask members of the class to look again at the famous Dürer monogram. Instruct them to create one for themselves to sign works of art, identify personal possessions, print on T-shirts, or put to other uses.

Or have them use the monogram to create a repeated pattern design with different sizes and/or colors. Display the monogram creations for all to see.

CONNECT 4: Duplicate copies of "The Venn Diagram" activity sheet for students or small groups. Remind the class of the woodcut printing that both Dürer and Hokusai did. Use that as a starter as they discuss and complete the parts of the diagram.

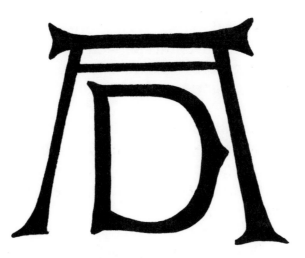

In the life of Diego Velásquez we see another artist who prized art and nature. He regarded them both as close friends. Diego was born in Seville, Spain, in 1599 of noble parents. By age 11 he had been apprenticed to an artist-historian, Pacheco. Eight years later Velásquez was himself a teacher to young apprentices.

In Velásquez's day portrait painters were highly regarded. Photography had not been invented yet and good portraits were used in arranging royal marriages. After Velásquez painted a portrait for Philip IV of Spain, Philip recognized his unusual talent and made him a court painter. Diego was given a salary and a studio in the Escorial near Madrid.

SPAIN

Peter Paul Rubens encouraged his friend Velásquez to travel to Italy to visit and learn more about art and artists. For more than a year Velásquez studied the works of Tintoretto and Titian as well as other famous painters. During subsequent similar trips Velásquez purchased for King Philip works that today are prized possessions of the Prado Museum in Madrid.

Diego Velásquez painted Philip's family with more affection and respect than had been given any other royal group. The king and his court painter became close friends. Velásquez eventually received the red cross of a Knight of Saint James, an out-of-the-ordinary honor for an artist.

Velásquez did several equestrian portraits portraying horses and riders with near perfection. But undoubtedly the most famous of Diego's works is *Las Meninas*, The Maids of Honor. It has been called "a towering achievement of world painting" and one of the most famous canvases in all the world.

CONNECT 1: Secure a copy of *Las Meninas*. Art history books or the school art department probably has one. Discuss with the class the people shown in this painting. Who is the center of attention? How many adults are there? How many children? Are the king and queen present? Who is standing behind the easel? What is the setting for the scene? (ANSWERS: Princess Margarita is getting the attention. Two dwarfs are at the right near the dog, two attendants are near the five-year-old princess, two others are seen in the shadows at the right, Velásquez himself is behind the easel, a palace officer stands in the doorway in the back. The royal parents are the subjects of the painting. They are opposite the princess, their reflections in the mirror near their daughter's head. All are shown in Velásquez's palace studio.)

CONNECT 2: Provide magazines to the students from which they can cut pictures. Ask cooperative-learning groups to select a character from *Las Meninas*. Instruct members to browse through the magazines to find what could be considered an up-to-date version of the original character. On a large sheet of paper, sketch an up-to-date palace studio scene. When the background is complete, group members should glue the "new" characters in their proper places. Ask students if Diego Velásquez would recognize this version if he should visit your class.

CONNECT 3: Remind your students of the honor Diego Velásquez received, the red cross of the Knight of Saint James. Ask for volunteers to write a short play in which they reenact this ceremony of honor.

Perhaps you can even create a proper award to be given to deserving students for tasks or services well done in your classroom. Rewrite the Knight's ceremony if necessary and use it at appropriate times in your room.

CONNECT 4: Duplicate copies of the "A Horse, Of Course" activity page. Ask those interested in equestrian history to research different breeds of horses. Perhaps a map could be created with homelands of the animals shown with small drawings of the breed. Students could expand the list also. Display final research with colored photos or drawings so everyone can enjoy the display. (Of course, include Velásquez's equestrian portraits as accent pieces.)

Although they lived thousands of miles apart, the Japanese artist Hokusai influenced the world of Europeans Paul Gauguin, Vincent Van Gogh, and Henri de Toulousse-Lautrec. These men considered Hokusai to be a master.

Hokusai lived from 1760-1849. Because his family was poor he started working at an early age. He was raised by a man who made metal mirrors. In his late teens he acquired skill in painting actors for performance on the stage. The expertise with which he performed his job earned him the name "Shunro." In Japanese tradition artists have the privilege of taking on new names as they change jobs or artistic styles. More than 40 times in his life Hokusai took on a new name.

As did Albrecht Dürer, Hokusai learned the art of woodblock printing. His prints provide glimpses of everyday scenes...people fishing, harvesting rice, traveling to market. Hokusai created words with trees and flowers, birds and insects, and machines and buildings.

Among his most unusual works are 36 different views of Mt. Fuji, a tiny painting of two birds on a single grain of rice, and one work so large that people had to view it from the roofs of buildings.

When he was 78, Hokusai lost all his sketches and record books when his house burned. Despite this tragedy he left 30,000 prints, sketches, and drawings.

Late in his life Hokusai wrote, "From the age of six I had a mania for drawing. At 73 I learned a little about the real structure of nature. When I am 80, I shall have made more progress. At 90 I shall penetrate the mystery of things. When I am 100 everything I do...will be alive." As he lay dying the "old man mad about art" said, "If heaven would grant me ten more years, I would become a real painter."

CONNECT 1: Hokusai's *Great Wave of Kanagawa* provides an excellent prelude for reading Pearl S. Buck's *Big Wave*. The works blend to create a memorable look at man's life in Japan as he struggles against nature.

Read this short story aloud to your class or assign it to groups of students to read and discuss.

CONNECT 2: Make a camera available to selected students for this project. Tell the group of the 36 different views of Mt. Fuji that Hokusai created. Select a meaningful object or place within reasonable distance of the classroom. Instruct the group to creatively photograph the subject to end up with 36 different views of their subject. When the film is developed, have the committee display their work with captions.

CONNECT 3: Students may wish to simulate Hokusai's woodblock printing. Use balsa for easy carving if it is available. If not, consider vegetable printing. Potatoes and carrots are firm yet easy to carve. Dipped in tempera, vegetables can make very colorful designs. Or try modeling clay for the printing and an inked stamp pad for ink. Students may select something contemporary or something more in the style of the Oriental prints Hokusai created. The finishing touch should be a signature stamp such as those seen in most works by Oriental artists.

CONNECT 4: Duplicate copies of the "Climbing Mt. Fuji" activity sheet. Some members of the class may wish to use colored pencils or paints to add color to the page. Challenge the cooperative-learning groups to find the most unusual and interesting events or characteristics connected with Fujiyama. As groups report to one another, offer students the option of adding to their list of five with outstanding ideas researched by classmates.

JUDITH LEYSTER

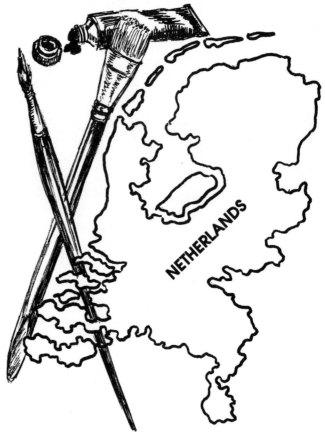

Judith Leyster was a seventeenth century Dutch artist. Her talents in art were recognized early in her life. By age 19 she was selling paintings.

Some of her early works were drawings of flowers made for advertising brochures for the growing tulip industry. In addition to flowers, Leyster painted still lifes and portraits to adorn private homes. (Hanging paintings in private homes was becoming very popular in the early 1600s in Holland.)

Frans Hals, a Dutch painter and a contemporary of Flemish artist Peter Paul Ruebens, was Judith Leyster's teacher. Due to his teaching Leyster refined her techniques of dramatic light and intense color. Both were artistic trends in wide use at the time.

By the time she was in her mid-twenties, she was teaching students of her own. Judith Leyster died in 1660.

CONNECT 1: Secure a copy of Judith Leyster's painting, *The Jester.* Your library or art department prints file may be good sources. Tell students that men like the jester were entertainers of the day, men who sang and danced in the town square and at the local taverns. Ask the class to find evidence of the dramatic lighting and intense color described on the previous page.

Have students turn to the music section of this book and the lesson on the lute and relate that instrument lesson to *The Jester.* He is holding the lute.

CONNECT 2: Secure a copy of Pablo Picasso's *Seated Harlequin.* Explain that the harlequin's occupation is similar to that of a jester. Have students compare and contrast the two paintings and the jobs the two men held.

Ask students to name men and women today who make their living playing instruments, singing, and entertaining the public. Discuss similarities and differences between the people and jobs today and those of 400 years ago.

CONNECT 3: Form small discussion groups for the purpose of sharing thoughts on what students think they might be doing when they are age 19. Remind the class that for a young female in the early 1600s (such as Judith Leyster) to have an established career at age 19 was remarkable. Ask students to speculate on what talents and education would have been necessary for such success in that field.

Take this idea one step further by asking students to find local teens who have achieved early success in their lives as Judith Leyster did. Have students interview them, then report back to the class describing how they were able to achieve their goals. Then the students can complete the "Where Am I Going?" activity sheet. Provide time for class discussion about setting goals and about the short- and long-term goals Judith Leyster might have set for herself as she was growing up.

Because the land shaped Greek life, the evolution of the Greek vase reflects the geography of Greece. The legend is told that the maker of the world was using a sieve to create the landscape. He sifted the soil and spread it here and there at varying depths. At last only stones were left in the sieve and the rocks were tossed at the water's edge. Greece came into being.

The peninsula is rocky and mountains divided early peoples. The limestone soil is thin and supports sparse vegetation and few grazing animals. Olive trees and grapes grow well here despite soil conditions.

No place in Greece is more than 85 miles from the sea. Early residents turned to the sea for resources, trading, and transportation. Commerce with neighboring lands and colonies grew as Greeks bought and sold olive oil, wine, and grain.

Containers were needed for everyday use, for merchants, and for temple decorations. The potter became a respected member of Greek society. The clay needed for creating vases was plentiful in salt marshes near the seas.

CONNECT 1: Display pictures or books showing samples of Greek pottery. Instruct cooperative-learning groups to create small samples of the most common types of vases. Fold three-inch squares of black construction paper in half. Sketch half a vessel. Cut to create a symmetrical silhouette of a Greek vase. Tell students they need to learn the name and purpose of the vessel they have created. Each member then teaches others in the group about his/her sample. If possible, have groups share with one another. Attach all small black samples to a sheet. Label them and set aside for future reference.

CONNECT 2: Select photos or drawings of Greek vases from research materials. Include kraters, amphoras, hydrias, a kylike (also kylix), a skyphos, a lekythos, or others. Describe, then discuss the details of the vessels, their possible uses, and any story depicted there. To close, have the class draw conclusions about how these common containers have become an invaluable view of life in ancient Greece.

CONNECT 3: Share with students that the Greeks were one of the first ancient societies to place value on the individual citizen no matter what his/her status. The Greeks also believed in living life in the present, rather than the present being a preparation for the next life.

Ask each class member to pick an attribute, a talent, an accomplishment about himself/herself. This positive quality will be displayed on a Greek vase style of the student's choosing. Each student can cut or draw figures to tell the story of the positive attribute on the paper vessel and use marker or paper to creatively decorate as the Greeks did. Borders and line designs should adorn the edges. Have each student share the finished products orally with the class. It is important that each student stand in front of others to tell about his/her talent or accomplishment.

CONNECT 4: Prepare copies of the puzzle "Vases, Vessels, Jugs, and Jars"...one per student or one per cooperative-learning group. Have students work the puzzle. There is an answer key provided in the back of this book.

FOLK ARTS - PAPER CRAFTS

Throughout the world, across time, folk artists have learned to rely heavily on talent while depending minimally on sophisticated materials. Skill and ingenuity were present whenever needed; supplies were sometimes difficult to acquire.

POLAND

Weed seeds, shells, tree bark, corn husks, fabric scraps, pine needles, and paper scraps were commonly used materials. Handcrafted projects created by ordinary folk are present in every world culture.

Studying the ethnic arts of a chosen culture and learning the purpose and construction of the objects can be an exciting experience for your students. German bells, amate paper cutouts of the Otomi Indians in Mexico, paper molas from the Cuna Indians of Panama, origami from the Orient, and Polish wycinanki (vi-chee-no-key) cutouts are a few examples you may wish to investigate.

As the class tries these Polish stars, encourage students to recognize that in addition to learning about other cultures through crafts they are joining the artisan in working with their hands, solving problems as they arise, helping one another achieve, and thinking critically and creatively in producing an aesthetically pleasing product.

POLISH STARS

1. On an 8¹/₂" x 11" sheet of white unlined paper create as large a circle as possible. Using this as a pattern, cut seven more.

2. Fold one circle in half, then in fourths, then in eighths. Open it. On each folded line mark a dot one inch from the center of the circle.

3. Lay all eight circles on top of one another. The folded, dotted pattern circle on top. Paper clip all eight circles in several places.

4. Starting at the outside of the stack of circles, cut on each folded line using the dot as a stop sign. Do NOT cut through to the center. Reposition paper clips as needed to hold all sheets securely to prevent slipping as you cut.

5. Working with one cut circle, pick up two edges, one between each thumb and forefinger. Curl inward on top of each other. Overlap until you have formed a tight, slender cone. Glue or tape securely. Repeat until 8 tight cones appear on the starter circle. Set aside. Repeat step 5 with all remaining circles. You will have produced 64 tight slender cones.

6. Create a base holder by cutting a circle the size of a 25-cent piece from heavy paper or thin cardboard. Poke two holes in it to resemble a button.

7. Thread a large needle with a yard of yarn or lightweight string. Knot one end. Then thread the yarn through the "button." Now string all 8 pointy circles. Tie securely on the top of the last circle. (HINT: Using the folded pattern circle as the last at the top works best.)

8. Use the remaining tail of string or yarn as a hanger. Display in groups at varying heights.

9. OTHER OPTIONS: Vary the size of the circles as you become adept at making Polish stars. Add glitter to tips for a decorative touch. Use printed wrapping paper or foil wrap for a festive change.

CHINESE OPERA MASKS

Imagine you are visiting in China, attending a special evening performance. Sights and sounds include pantomime, music, martial arts, singing, dialogue among the performers, and acrobatics. Can you guess where you would be able to see and hear all this entertainment in one setting? It is the Chinese opera. As you can imagine, it is not easy being an opera performer and being required to be proficient in all these areas.

Much of the acting in Chinese opera is symbolic, with body and footwork giving clues to action and story. Body language and pantomime give visual effects of riding a horse, climbing stairs, or pulling a cart. Nothing is done casually. The slightest movement of hands, eyes, or mouth is highly significant.

The musicians are on stage with the actors rather than being in a pit off stage as in America. Instruments used include an organ with reed pipes, a mandolin, fiddles with two strings, the Chinese lute, bells, gongs, castanets, drums, and the clarinet. Many times the melodies are improvised during the performances depending on the action on stage and the message intended to be conveyed to the audience.

Dating back to the times when operatic stories were performed in the open air, makeup is bright and heavy. It is applied all over the face and is greatly exaggerated. For example, the handsome energetic face of the jing actor has eyebrows pointed upward signifying energy. (Jing are actors or singers who represent warriors, demons, heroes, or statesmen.) The clown has white paint around his nose and eyes. Audiences familiar with the operas and their stories can distinguish characters simply by their face paint.

Clothing worn for the Chinese opera is beautifully embroidered with bright colors. Special hats and jewelry are also used. The costumes are sophisticated yet comfortable, allowing for freedom of movement for the agile actors and actresses.

CONNECT 1: Distribute copies of the "Chinese Opera Masks" activity sheet. After viewing the samples, encourage the class to use creative originality in the construction of their own masks.

Start with a pattern that is the shape and size of the student's face. Have students use partners to help trace one side of the face, then fold and cut to produce a symmetrical mask. Then they can mark and cut holes for eyes, a slit for the nose, and an open space for the mouth.

Encourage students to use plenty of unusual, colorful shapes to represent the makeup, and to add hair, headdresses, beards, and other touches for a unique mask.

CONNECT 2: Students can use the masks above in a play written by someone in the group or in performing a story from Chinese literature.

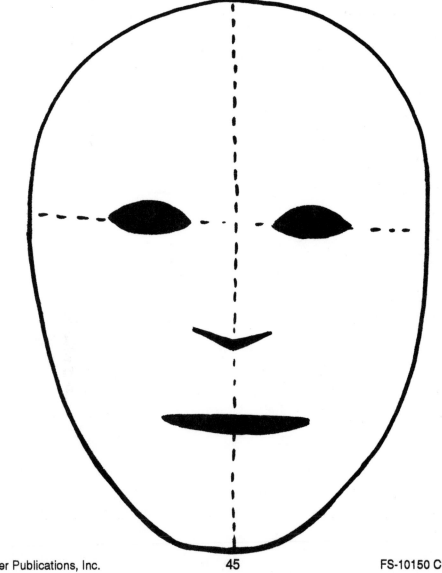

Name: _____

Use this art criticism sheet each time you explore a work of art. Check words that describe what you discover as you view the artist's work. The opinion section serves to summarize what you have learned.

ART CRITICISM

Painting _____
Artist _____

Check words that describe this painting.

LINES		COLORS		LIGHT AND DARK	
choppy	_____	bright	_____	Squint your eyes and	
curved	_____	strong	_____	look at the painting.	
diagonal	_____	soft	_____	Where is the most	
fuzzy	_____	dark	_____	light?	
heavy	_____	warm	_____	right	_____
horizontal	_____	cool	_____	left	_____
jagged	_____	neutral	_____	top	_____
sharp	_____	-------------------------		middle	_____
straight	_____	**TEXTURES**		bottom	_____
thick	_____	dull	_____	Where is the most	
thin	_____	shiny	_____	dark?	
vertical	_____	soft	_____	right	_____
-------------------------		hard	_____	left	_____
SHAPES		rough	_____	top	_____
angular	_____	smooth	_____	middle	_____
circular	_____	-------------------------		bottom	_____
curved	_____	**OBJECTS**		-------------------------	
hard-edged	_____	people	_____	**OPINION**	
soft-edged	_____	animals	_____	I like these things	
square	_____	trees	_____	about this painting...	
rectangular	_____	buildings	_____		
triangular	_____	sky	_____		
-------------------------		water	_____	I dislike these things	
BALANCE		food	_____	about this work...	
symmetrical	_____	no objects	_____		
asymmetrical	_____				

UNFINISHED PAINTING

This is all of the green-faced man Chagall painted in *I and the Village*.
Finish the drawing and add color. Do you prefer the finished face or
Marc Chagall's version? If you would like, create the remainder of this
man, sharing the complete person with your classmates.

THE VENN DIAGRAM

Review the biographies of German artist, Albrecht Dürer and Katsushika Hokusai, the Japanese artist. Write phrases in all three parts of the Venn diagram to compare and contrast the lives of these men.

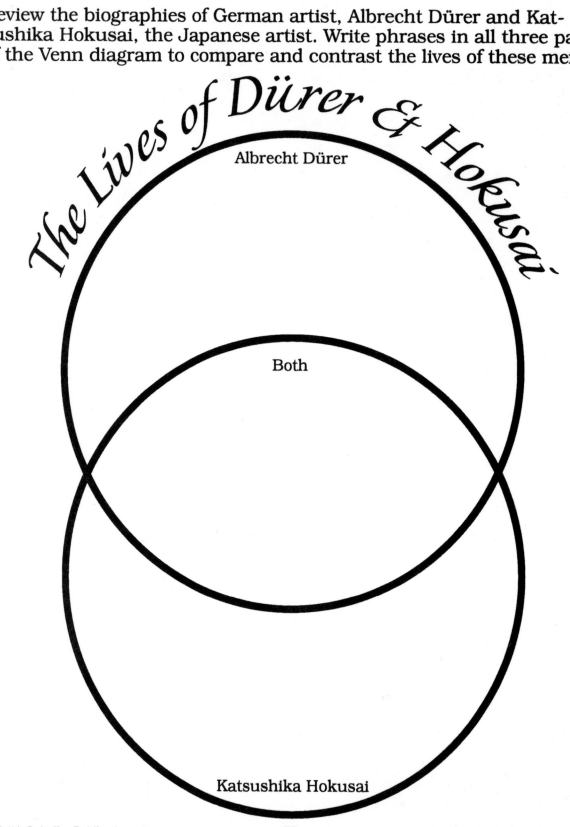

The Lives of Dürer & Hokusai

Albrecht Dürer

Both

Katsushika Hokusai

Name: _____

A HORSE, OF COURSE

Listed below are some of the many breeds of horses found in different parts of the world. The development of these specialized animals gives clues to climate, topography, and occupations found in the horses' homelands. Choose one or several of the suggestions here or supply your own breeds. Write, draw pictures, create puzzles, or use other methods to share ideas you have gained in research.

Arabian
Icelandic Pony

Welsh
Percheron
Lippizaner

Belgian
Shetland

49

Name: _____

CLIMBING MT. FUJI

Mt. Fuji is a mountain sacred to the Japanese as well as the nation's highest peak. Organize a research project in which your cooperative-learning group challenges another to find five of the most unusual characteristics or events connected with this mountain. Write your finalized set on the mountain. Add paint for a colorful touch.

WHERE AM I GOING?

GOAL SETTING provides helpful direction for simple and involved accomplishments. A few minutes taken to put thoughts on paper can be rewarding as short- and long-term tasks are fulfilled.

What goals are you working on at the present? Write the objective above the arrow. Then fill in the boxes on the right. Use this sheet as many times as you like.

SET GOALS FOR...

ONE DAY

What is needed to achieve my goal?

How will I know I have reached my goal?

ONE WEEK

What is needed to achieve my goal?

How will I know I have reached my goal?

ONE MONTH

What is needed to achieve my goal?

How will I know I have reached my goal?

VASES, VESSELS, JUGS, AND JARS

Review what you have learned about Greek vases by completing the puzzle below. Place a letter on each space to correctly spell the name of the vase pictured. When done, you will have completed a phrase in the vertical boxes.

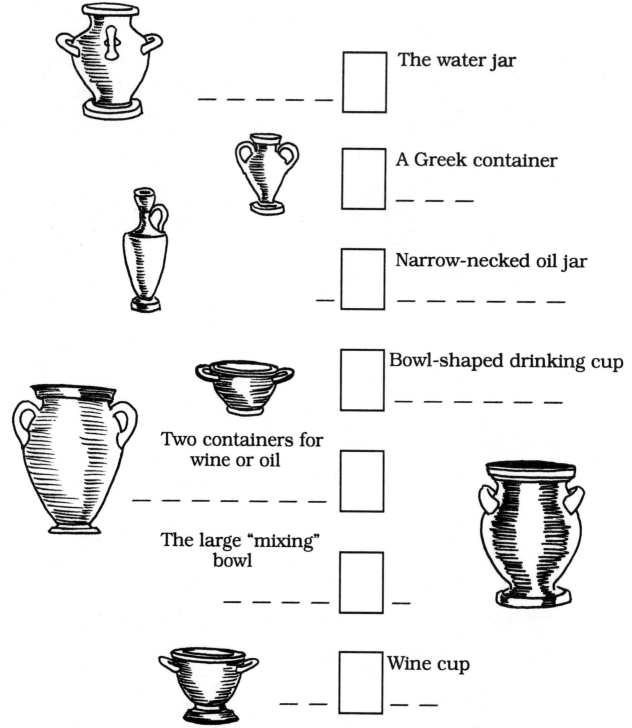

The water jar

A Greek container

Narrow-necked oil jar

Bowl-shaped drinking cup

Two containers for wine or oil

The large "mixing" bowl

Wine cup

CHINESE OPERA MASKS

Study these pictures to learn more about Chinese opera masks. Determine which features you wish to include in your own production.

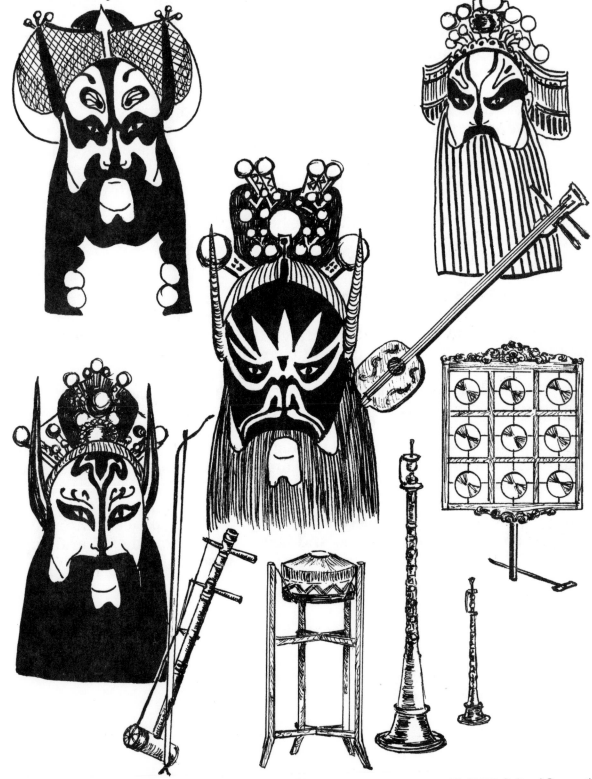

CHAPTER 3
MUSIC MAKERS

The origins of music and musical instruments are indefinite. Historians agree that music, like other cultural elements, was intertwined with stories, religion, mathematics, even astronomy. Researchers are equally certain that later civilizations "borrowed" from earlier groups, creating similarities and overlapping among cultures.

From art work on temple walls, stone carvings, and pottery we learn about musical instruments of long ago. Writings of later peoples describe dance, theater, and festivals in which music played a part. Occasionally musical instruments found in the tombs of people of ancient civilizations have been discovered in a condition that allows them to be played today.

Singing may have begun by imitating the sounds of animals or simply as a form of communication. A third theory suggests music may have developed from work rhythms and chants.

The first musical instruments were probably adaptations of work tools and other useful instruments. No doubt rhythm instruments developed before melodic ones. People's life styles dictated the kind of music makers and how they were used. For instance, flutes were common among herders and pastoral peoples. Nomadic peoples developed easily portable instruments. More settled groups with many resources had a wide variety of instruments made from their wide variety of materials.

A few instruments seem common among many cultures—rattles, drums, animal horns or shells, thumb pianos and jew's harps, xylophones, and gongs to name a few.

To know a culture's music makers is to know how people communicated, how people used familiar objects, and how they developed skill and sophistication in the creation of music and musical instruments.

The *balalaika* (baa lay lik uh) is a chordophone, meaning it has strings to produce tones. It is a member of the guitar family but is triangular in shape. The back is flat, the belly is slightly arched. It has a long, narrow neck with four frets that are movable. The balalaika usually has three or four strings made of gut, but some models have steel strings. It can be tuned several ways. Its sound is similar to a mandolin, but is a bit softer.

It is believed that the Tatar tribes of the Russian province probably invented this instrument. It seems to be a descendant of the dombra, an instrument already common in Russia in the sixteenth century. The balalaika made its appearance sometime in the eighteenth century.

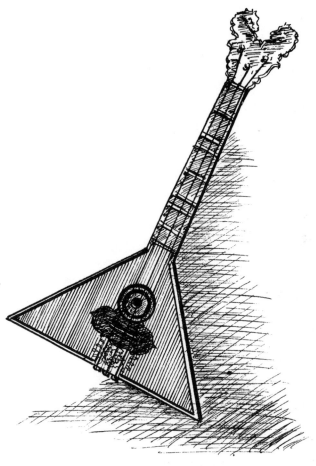

The balalaika was improved by V. V. Andreyev. Its six sizes include a piccolo model, a prime, a second, an alto, a bass, and a contrabass. This last model is so large it must rest upon the floor as it is played. The prime is the most common model. After the Russian Revolution in 1917, whole balalaika orchestras including all sizes were commonly heard in Europe and America.

There is evidence that some people in northeast Siberia still play the two-stringed version (common until the late seventeenth century). According to folklore the Buryat hunters of Siberia sing and play their balalaikas to entertain the spirits of the forest.

CONNECT 1: Have students investigate the possibility of a music library or a music instructor providing a recording of Russian balalaika music to which they can listen. Share information that may be included with the music.

CONNECT 2: Have members of the class recreate a balalaika family of instruments including the piccolo balalaika, the prime, the second, the alto, the bass, and the contrabass. They may use a format of their choice. Ideas include painted illustrations, miniature models, life-size models, or clay sculptures.

CONNECT 3: The shape of the balalaika is simple and geometric. Assign one student to use computer graphics to recreate a balalaika on his/her computer. Share the coordinates so others can reproduce the graphic.

CONNECT 4: Prepare as if a traveling musical group from Russia were visiting an auditorium in your area. Students can design a poster advertising the visit. It should tell where the group is from, what type of concert music they will perform, show what the instrument looks like, and give necessary details for the concert—time, place, and cost.

The bagpipe is so ancient an instrument, it is impossible to determine where it originated. It seems to have been invented independently in many countries around the world. It is a solo, melodic, unison instrument never intended to be played with other instruments in harmony or in an orchestra.

The bagpipe is a wind instrument in which air is stored in a bladder or bag to provide continuous sound. Air enters the bag via the blowpipe. The nonreturn valve serves to keep air within the bag. The chanter is another pipe attached opposite the blowpipe. It has a double reed and eight open holes (seven on the front and one on the back). The melody is played here with both hands. The three drone pipes are fitted with double reeds. Early models of the bagpipe had one, two, or three drone pipes. The drone is almost always tuned two octaves below the key note of the chanter.

The role of the bagpipe is one of the most varied of all instruments in history. It has been used by shepherds as they tended sheep, for weddings and funerals, to amuse noblemen, as accompaniment for dances, and to mark time for military groups. And in 1755 Mozart included a bagpipe in his orchestra for the music for *Peasant Wedding.*

Although ancient Romans, Persians, Turks, Palestinians, Irish, Spanish, Indians, and French have all had their own versions of the bagpipe, it is considered the national instrument of the people of Scotland.

CONNECT 1: If possible, secure a copy of *Music* from the *Eyewitness Books* series, authored by Neil Ardley. It has marvelous pictures of Hungarian and French bagpipes that can be an interesting comparison/contrast visual and oral lesson for the class.

CONNECT 2: Secure a copy of Pieter Breughel's *Children's Games* painting. Encourage students to locate the bagpipe player and then go on to count the 80 (or at least some of them) games depicted in this marvelous painting.

CONNECT 3: There are many similarities between bagpipes and accordions. Assign a group of students to use a Venn diagram with pictures and phrases to compare these two instruments.

CONNECT 4: Dance and music go hand in hand. Secure a recording of bagpipe music to use as background sound for demonstrating the steps to the highland fling. A physical education teacher in your school or a dance instructor in the community might serve as a resource person for this activity.

ALPENHORN

Since prehistoric times the long, wooden alpenhorn (or alphorn) has echoed across the mountains of Switzerland. The first horns were bored from a log to make the instrument used for signalling among mountain herders. Later designs retained the long tube shape but were made of long wooden staves bound tightly with birchbark strips.

Sizes of alpenhorns vary from 5 feet (1 1/2 m) to 13 feet (4 m). This difference, of course, causes variations in pitch.

The alpenhorn eventually was used for simple melodies as well as for signaling. It is a member of the trumpet family of instruments. Those who constructed alpenhorns also experimented with various mouthpieces. Even so, they remained cup-shaped and made of wood.

The most common use of the alpenhorn today is for tourists who wish to hear its powerful tones cross Swiss valleys. On occasion it is still heard today in the *William Tell* opera by Gioacchino Rossini.

         FS-10150 Cultural Connections

CONNECT 1: Instruct students to use simple or easily accessible materials to experiment with producing different sounds from tubes of different lengths. In this way they can see why alpenhorns varied so in size. Bottles with water could also be used for this investigation.

CONNECT 2: Add alpenhorn to the "Choose a Music Maker" activity sheet included in this section. Perhaps cooperative-learning groups could construct a whole family of alpenhorns.

CONNECT 3: Ask the class to compare and contrast the alpenhorn with the Tibetan Buddhist sacred trumpet in the following categories: use, looks, sound, and construction.

CONNECT 4: Have a group of students use the costumed character dressed in native attire and create a diorama depicting a Swiss person playing an alpenhorn. The background scene, of course, should be of the Alps.

CONNECT 5: While we have concentrated here on the folk instrument alpenhorn, many other instruments are favorites of the Swiss people. Each student can write a report describing other popular music makers from Swiss history. Pictures can be included, too.

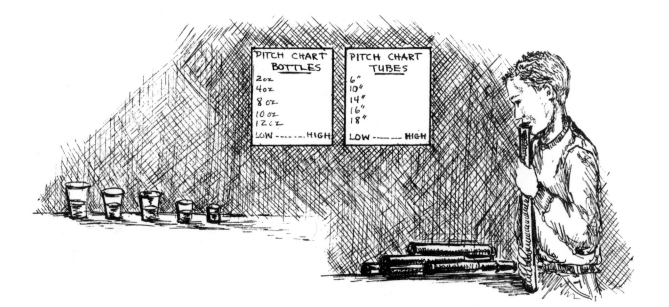

JAPANESE SAMISEN AND SHAKUHACHI

The *samisen* is the long-necked lute of Japan. Its square body is preferably made of mulberry, Chinese quince, or sandalwood. The belly and bottom are usually made of catskin. Its forerunner from China was round with a snakeskin belly and bottom, but the latter material did not stand up well when played with the Japanese plectrum (pick), so the more substantial material became more common. In addition, the body of the Chinese san hsien (three strings) was round. For quite some time the Japanese played their san gen (three strings) with a tsume (pick). Shape, materials, and name all changed as it evolved as a Japanese instrument.

The total length of the samisen is 94 cm (37 inches) with 74 cm (29 inches) in the neck.

The samisen is fretless. Its three strings have various tunings, two rather interesting ones used for comic music. The player uses a bone pick called a bachi to strike the belly (reinforced with parchment). The bachi's striking edge is 9 cm (3½ inches) wide at the head.

This instrument is still used today, particularly in Kabuki theater dramas where traditional music is an important element in the story being told.

Another instrument borrowed from their Chinese neighbors by the Japanese was the classical notched flute, the *shakuhachi.* It arrived from China in the early 900s. Japanese Buddhist priests carried and played the shakuhachi but, because of its shape and design, it was often used as a weapon by otherwise peaceable priests. The shakuhachi is made of bamboo and is lacquered, especially on the inside for protection from the moisture in the breath of the player. It has four fingerholes on the front and one in the back. There is a slight flare at the end opposite the mouthpiece. The standard size is 54.5 cm (about 21½ inches).

CONNECT 1: The Japanese samisen is similar to the American banjo, introduced to the New World by African Americans in the nineteenth century. Ask students to create charts, pictures, or other visual aids to compare the two instruments. Perhaps there is someone in your community who could visit the classroom and demonstrate one or both of these musical instruments.

If students are interested in the banjo, ask them to research the following: tenor, bass, and contra bass banjos, banjolin, banjo-mandolin, banjorine, or zither-banjo.

CONNECT 2: Add the samisen and shakuhachi to the "Choose a Music Maker" activity sheet included in this section. Assign this pair of Japanese music makers to a cooperative-learning group for illustration or construction. Add them to the growing instrument comparison group.

CONNECT 3: Ask students to create a cartoon in which the characters are a personified shakuhachi and a samisen. They are trying to settle an argument about which one is the more useful instrument. A touch of humor could be added here.

CONNECT 4: Most middle grade music textbooks have samples of music from Japan. Ask for a few student volunteers to locate, practice, and perform some Japanese music either through singing or by playing an instrument. They can ask a music instructor for assistance if they need help with this presentation.

CONNECT 5: Ask each student to submit a sample of a postage stamp honoring Japanese musical instruments. Submit the designs to the whole class for voting. Enlarge the winning design and "post" it in the room.

CHINESE PIPA

Chinese music has a long tradition reaching back into time some 4,000 years. China's history records ancient orchestras or groups of instrument players. They received the pitch to tune their instruments from a sacred gong called the huang chung. Instruments were divided into eight categories based on the type of material from which they were constructed. Instruments themselves were then related to such things as seasons, points on the compass, and aspects of nature like thunder, fire, or water.

The Chinese used the five note pentatonic scale. Those notes are F, G, A, C, and D. To hear these sounds, play a grouping of black notes on the piano. There is no harmony in Chinese music.

The *pipa*, (also called pi pa or pyipar) is a type of short-necked lute. It is approximately 36–40 inches long (90 cm–l m) and 15 inches (39 cm) wide. It has four strings tuned in fourths. Melodies are usually played on the highest string. It is held in an upright position resting on the player's thigh. It is plucked with bare fingers. The companion instrument known as the jin or yue qin, similar to a mandolin, is also played by plucking.

The pipa is recorded in literature of the second century A.D. It is believed this instrument may have come to China from nomads of Central Asia. Its size and shape made the pipa convenient to play from horseback. The Japanese instrument biwa descended from the Chinese pipa.

CONNECT 1: After his visit to the Orient, Marco Polo wrote a book so that all people would know what he discovered in those faraway lands. Have the class create a play in which Marco Polo recounts his first experience in the presence of the Khans where he hears Chinese instruments played. They can use models of the instruments in addition to usual props, simple or complex. You might want to divide the class into three groups who could write, direct, and produce a look back at ancient Chinese music through drama.

CONNECT 2: Students should add pipa to the "Choose a Music Maker" activity sheet included in this section. Ask a cooperative group or an individual to illustrate or construct an ancient Chinese lute to be included in the comparison display of instruments from different cultures.

CONNECT 3: Students can use the dimensions given in this section to create a Chinese pipa from cardboard or draw one to scale on a sheet of paper. Display the instruments in the room.

CONNECT 4: Locate pictures of several members of the lute family from different nations of the world. Ask each cooperative-learning group to select a different model to draw. They should create a family of lutes, show their nation of origin on a world map, and make the flag of the nation to which the lute belongs. Display the music makers, the flags, and the world map for all to see.

CONNECT 5: Have each student write a poem in first person, the "person" being a Chinese pipa that is part of an opera orchestra. Each poem should describe the role the pipa plays on stage during the performance. The theme of the opera is the story of an evil prince who must give up his throne as a result of all the evil things he has done.

INDIAN SITAR

The *sitar* was originated by Amir Khusro, a poet and singer who lived in the thirteenth century. Its name comes from the Persian word *sehtar* meaning three-stringed. The sitar belongs to the lute family. Most often it is made from a seasoned gourd that serves as its resonating chamber. Teakwood is often used for the neck. The neck piece is three inches (7 ½ cm) wide. This neck carries a flat fingerboard with 16–20 movable frets made either of brass, silver, or gut.

There are six or seven main strings, four of which are played. The remaining two or three are rhythm or drone strings. The main strings are tuned and plucked with a plectrum (a pick) called a *mizrab*. It is worn on the index finger of the right hand.

Along the hollow neck and below the main strings are 13 sympathetic strings. These strings are tuned and vibrate to the sound of the main strings. Occasionally the player reaches between the main strings with the little finger to pluck the sympathetic strings. This allows for conforming to the scale of a particular *raga* (traditional form of Hindu music).

A partner to the Indian sitar is the *tambura*. It is similar to the sitar but has no frets and has just four strings. The tambura's sole purpose is to provide a drone background. The single melodic line in Indian music is never harmonized. Elaborate drum rhythms embellish it. The seven notes of the Indian scale are *sa, re, ga, ma, pa, dha,* and *ni.*

CULTURAL CONNECTIONS

CONNECT 1: Two other instruments make interesting comparison/contrast situations. Ask a committee to compare the Bedouin instrument *zummara* with the Indian snake charmer's (known as a *pungi*) *tiktiri*. The tiktiri is a sort of double clarinet with two cane pipes within a gourd. The zummara is descended from the ancient instrument called a *memet* and is also a double clarinet.

CONNECT 2: Assign a committee to ask the art instructor or use the reference section in the library to locate samples of ancient Indian art. They can visually explore, searching for costumes, customs, and musical instruments. In how many examples is the sitar seen?

CONNECT 3: Students can add the sitar to the "Choose a Music Maker" activity sheet included in this section. Assign this Indian music maker to a group for illustration or the construction aspect of this musical instrument comparison series.

CONNECT 4: Other than the sitar, traditional Indian instruments include the *sarangi* (a form of fiddle), the *diruba* (a blend of sitar and sarangi), the *vina* (a type of lute), the *tambura* (an unfretted, long lute), and the *tiktiri* (a double clarinet). Tell students they are in charge of an instrument display for a music store window. They may wish to create a poster-size drawing of the storefront with the instruments in place and label them so that they can be easily identified.

CONNECT 5: Music creates sounds but not all sounds are music. Have the class imagine sounds one might hear on a busy street in a large city in India. Then ask a group of students to reproduce those sounds to sound as "real" as possible and then record the sounds on tape. Students may create a rhythmic pattern (hands beating on desk top, drum stick on glass) to accompany the recording and perform the unmusical music for the class.

THE LUTE

The *lute* is an ancient instrument that probably originated in the Caucasus Mountains near the Caspian Sea. Mesopotamian art work dating to 1600 B.C. portrays men playing the lute. One hundred years later a female lute player appeared on a Cretan bowl. In Egypt the lute seems to have been played only by women. The next appearance was on Greek vases. From the Greeks this instrument made its way to the Romans. After the Middle Ages the playing of the lute rapidly spread (along with many other ideas) throughout Europe. The ancestor of our Western lute is the sixth century Arabic al'ud (lute). By the fifteenth century the plectrum (pick) formerly used to play the lute was abandoned.

The lute is a chordophone (strings as the sound-producing element). It has a flat neck with seven or more frets. The pegbox is bent back at an angle. It has a hollow, pear-shaped body. When it first appeared the lute had 5-6 strings but as it changed during time, 9-11 became the most common number. The three-stringed version still appears in northwest Africa today.

Lutes were made from a wide variety of woods, ebony, ivory, and whalebones, although ivory and whalebone instruments were considered to have inferior tone. The woods used included maple, yew, sycamore, oak, plum, and cherry.

This ancestor of the guitar and violin came in short- and long-necked versions. Lightweight despite the size of the resonance cavity, sizes ranged from 12–60 inches. An example from 1500 B.C. was 62 cm (24 ½") long. A Chinese lute dating from A.D. 200 was 90 cm (3' 5") long. A Turkish model was 106 cm (42") long, and a bass lute's size had a total length of 147 cm (58") with its body 95 cm (37 ½") long.

There were both bowed and plucked versions of the lute. It is a quiet, very expressive instrument tuned in fourths and thirds. The loveliness of the lute's appearance inspired those who constructed these instruments through the ages.

Music for the lute was written in *tablature*, a system of notation in which symbols of letters and/or numbers were used instead of notes. The earliest books of music for the lute were in Italian.

The lute was part of the Baroque music style and often accompanied the voice. In the sixteenth century every musician had a lute in his home. J. S. Bach composed some music for the lute. Recent efforts to revive the use of the lute have failed largely because players spend more time tuning than playing this instrument.

CONNECT 1: Have students return to the reproduction of Judith Leyster's *Jester*, and reread the printed descriptions given with her painting. Discuss which of the materials given in the text above might have been used to make the lute painted by Leyster. Finish the discussion with a recording of lute music if it is available.

CONNECT 2: Add the lute to the "Choose a Music Maker" activity sheet included in this section. Assign the lute to an individual or group for illustration or construction. Add this ancient instrument to the two-D or three-D display in the classroom.

CONNECT 3: Many nations around the world have variations of the lute. Draw the shape of a tree on posterboard and place the ancient lute on the trunk of the tree. On the branches, have students draw the instruments that have evolved from the original and use the names of the nations near the lute forms to identify the homes of these music makers.

CONNECT 4: Ask individual students or groups of students to write an original folktale in which a magical lute plays a leading role.

CONNECT 5: The lute was an important part of Baroque style. Baroque styles spilled over into art and architecture. Have groups of students investigate musical, artistic, and architectural examples of Baroque creations. Are there common elements among these three different areas? Have each group share its findings with the class in a format of its choosing.

DRUMS OF ALL CULTURES

In one form or another drums have been played all over the world throughout history. Their exact age is unknown but evidence of their existence can be dated to 3000 B.C. Drums were used as symbols of power and royalty, for magic, and for imitating thunder. One primitive type was made from skin stretched across an open pit. Sometimes pots were placed inside the pit to enhance the sound.

Early in the development of this chief percussion instrument, it was discovered that the greater the diameter the deeper the sound it produced, and the greater the tension placed on the membrane, the higher the pitch. But regardless of the size or form of the early drums, they were all struck with the players' hands.

Drums belong to the family called *membranophone*, that is, sound is produced when a membrane of some sort is stretched across a frame or surface. Only the Australians have no membrane drums. There are three main categories of drums—*tubular, vessel-shaped*, and *frame*. Within these groups are numerous examples, most of which are found all over the world.

Frame Drums:
Frame drums appear in art from Mesopotamia. The Israeli frame drum is called a *tof*. The European frame drum used in Greece, only by women, was called a *tympanon*. It was passed to the Romans where its name was *typanum*. These early frame drums had, at first, one head. The Romans introduced the double-headed version. The membrane was glued, nailed, or laced into place. Japanese frame drums used today are still constructed in this fashion. *Shamanic* drums (used for magic and religion) were used in many early cultures. Striking similarities in shamanic drums are found among the American Indians, the Lapps of northern Scandinavia, and the peoples of northern Siberia.

Cylinder Drums:

This style can be traced only to 2000 B.C. They were popular in China, less so among people of Southeast Asia. The latter seemed to have preferred gongs. There are some pottery drums of cylindrical style found among early American cultures. Those of the people of the southwestern United States were made of cottonwood and were used for war and dance drums. The height of these cylinder drums was twice that of the diameter.

Hourglass:

This style was two portable drums with cuplike sections joined to form a waist. Among the Berbers of north Africa, women were the chief players of the hourglass drum. They appeared in India as early as the second century B.C. The Chinese used this type of drum and passed it on to the Japanese via the Koreans.

Conical:

The ancient Mesopotamians used conical drums made of clay. A South African version was designed with open bottoms. These were played only by women. The Polynesians use their generic name *pahu* for all their membranophones. The conical pahu was made with wood from the breadfruit tree or from a coconut palm. It usually had a single head laced in place with sharkskin.

Goblet:

The goblet drum was common among Arab peoples ranging from Morocco to Iran. This type also was found as far north as Bulgaria. Samples appear on plaques dating from 1100 B.C. On these plaques the ovoid drums are seen on a stem reaching from the ground to the player's waist, as much as three feet.

Barrel:

This drum is wide at the center, has a round outline, and is narrow at the ends. It usually lies in a horizontal position and is struck on both ends when played. Long ago rice and other grain barrels in China were converted to musical instruments. This idea also passed through Korea to the Japanese, eventually. Today this ancient barrel drum idea is "alive and well" in the form of the Indian *mridanga*, where it is played with wrists and fingertips.

Rattledrums:

These are actually shaken membranophones. The Chinese rattledrum is called *t' ao-ku*. It is similar to the Asian Indian rattledrum. It is half drum and half rattle. By twirling the handle of the small drum, the attached beads strike the drum to produce the sound. Also called clapper or pellet drums, the attached objects may be glass beads, knots, or wax pellets.

Waterdrums:

Both North and South American peoples used water drums as ceremonial objects. They were made of wood or pottery and filled with water. The dull sound heard closeup carried well with the water inside the vessel. The heads of water drums were made with wetted, tanned buckskin and this facilitated the carrying power of the tone.

Kettledrums:

Kettledrums are hemispheric drums with bowls or basins. They are found on all continents as well as in the cultures of peoples in the Pacific. Among all peoples this drum shared these characteristics:

> It was a symbol of royalty.
> It was associated with trumpets.
> Small ones were always played in pairs.

The Islamic world introduced this drum to the Europeans. Crusaders returning from their journeys to the Mideast shared them. Use of horse-borne kettledrums was recorded in 1457 when the king of Hungary sent an embassy to France and used this instrument as part of the ceremony. In Russia, kettledrums were used to sound the signal alarm for fire fighters.

Friction Drums:

Sound is produced on this percussion instrument by a method other than striking. African cultures used hide to "scratch" the head of this drum to produce sound. Or, a cord or stick could be passed through the membrane. The origin of this friction drum may be in folklore or possibly from a child's toy. Often great ingenuity was displayed by the user of the friction drum. A tin cylinder type with a resined cord called a *locust* was sold in the early 1800s in Philadelphia. A German model with horsehair string was named *forest devil*. In India and Hawaii gourds or nuts with friction cords are used. In parts of Europe a cardboard box with cord produces the sound. Romanians use them in New Year's celebrations. Franz Hals painted *Man with the Rommelplot* depicting the Dutch version of the friction drum.

CONNECT 1: Locate the Franz Hals painting mentioned on the previous page. Study and discuss the instrument portrayed there. Also locate the famous painting of the American War of Independence, *1776*, showing three soldiers playing fife and drums. Send students on a treasure hunt among art books to locate several other examples of early instruments preserved for us in works of art.

CONNECT 2: Have students add the most interesting examples of the drum family to the instruments being illustrated or constructed for the room display. Another variation would be for a group of students to create the entire group discussed here. They could then create a display of ancient instruments for others to study. Modern percussion samples could provide an interesting contrast to the student display.

CONNECT 3: Ask class members to select examples from the drum family that can be reproduced with materials readily at hand (ice cream buckets, margarine containers, or oatmeal boxes). The *Music* volume of the *Eyewitness Book Series* by Neil Ardley has quality pictures to study. Let students experiment with the way the homemade drums can be changed to vary the sound. Permit students to borrow actual drums to bring to the classroom, and compare the sounds of the homemade music makers with the professionally manufactured ones.

CONNECT 4: Get in touch with a student in your school who plays a trap set. Ask if he or she can visit your classroom with the set of percussion instruments to demonstrate how one person learns to coordinate the playing of all parts of the set.

CONNECT 5: Electronics will probably produce much of our music of the future. Ask a student volunteer to interview someone who can share some of the latest developments in this field. The volunteer should be certain to inquire about electronic drum pads and then relay to classmates what he/she has learned.

CHOOSE A MUSIC MAKER

Fill each section below with the name of the instrument that fits the description given. Also draw a small picture that will give others an idea of the instrument's appearance.

Be able to defend your choices.

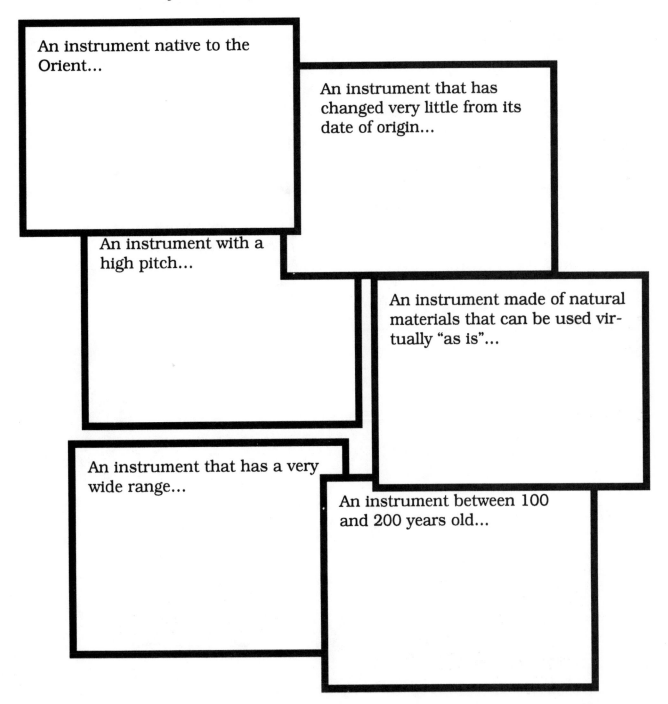

An instrument native to the Orient...

An instrument that has changed very little from its date of origin...

An instrument with a high pitch...

An instrument made of natural materials that can be used virtually "as is"...

An instrument that has a very wide range...

An instrument between 100 and 200 years old...

A NEW INVENTION

Follow these steps to invent a one-of-a-kind musical instrument.

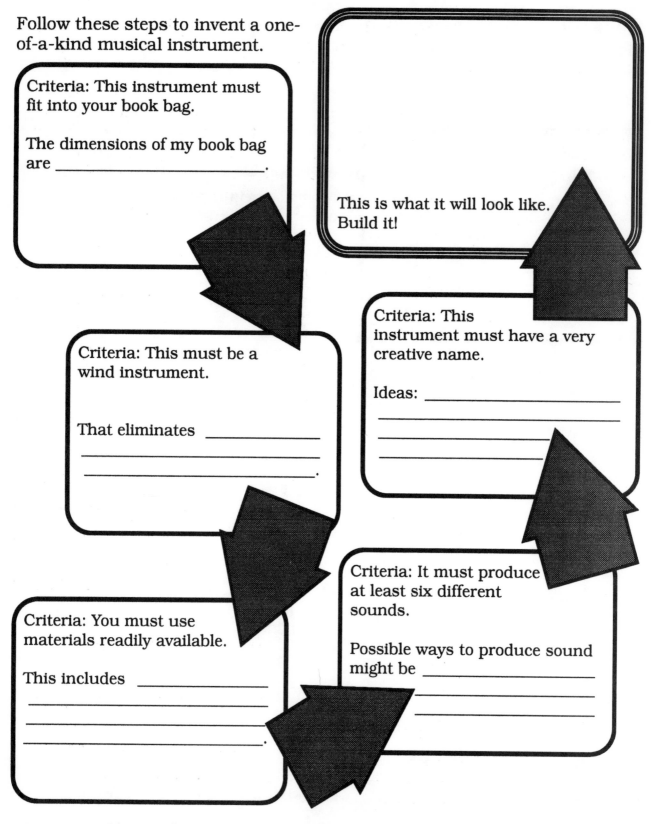

Criteria: This instrument must fit into your book bag.

The dimensions of my book bag are _____.

This is what it will look like. Build it!

Criteria: This must be a wind instrument.

That eliminates _____
_____
_____.

Criteria: This instrument must have a very creative name.

Ideas: _____
_____
_____
_____

Criteria: You must use materials readily available.

This includes _____
_____
_____
_____.

Criteria: It must produce at least six different sounds.

Possible ways to produce sound might be _____
_____
_____

Name: _____

GUIDING THE READER

Reader's Guide to Periodical Literature is a reference source designed to help in locating material printed in magazines that are issued periodically. It is more current than books and encyclopedias, making it an excellent source for up-to-date information.

Select a topic related to music of today, something in which you have interest. Use *Reader's Guide to Periodical Literature* to scan at least two articles related to your topic. (Ask the librarian if you need assistance.) Jot down notes in the spaces provided. Then write a half-page report using the information you find. Share your composition with the class.

PERIODICAL _____	PERIODICAL _____
_____	_____
AUTHOR_____	AUTHOR_____
ARTICLE TITLE _____	ARTICLE TITLE _____
_____	_____
VOLUME, DATE, PAGES _____	VOLUME, DATE, PAGES _____
_____	_____
NOTES: _____	NOTES: _____
_____	_____
_____	_____
_____	_____
_____	_____
_____	_____
_____	_____
_____	_____
_____	_____
_____	_____
_____	_____
_____	_____

ALLURING ALLITERATIONS

Have fun with the musical instruments discussed in this section and practice your writing skills in creating *alliterations*. Creative alliterations make great tongue twisters.

Here is an example to help you get started.

Paul plunked passionately upon the piano providing people powerful patterns.

Lute
Bagpipe
Alpenhorn
Drums
Sitar
P' ip' a
Balalaika

BE A MATCHMAKER

Be a matchmaker by placing each letter from the right column in the correct blank on the left. Reference materials will assist you as you learn more about musical instruments.

_____	1. A double-reeded instrument	A. recorder
_____	2. An instrument to shake	B. trombone
_____	3. Instruments designed to be struck	C. harp
_____	4. Similar to the trumpet	D. cornu
_____	5. Instrument played by plucking	E. fiddle
_____	6. Gamelan orchestra	F. cimbalom
_____	7. Ancient Roman war horn	G. clavichord
_____	8. Instrument with a slide	H. percussion
_____	9. A relative to the medieval rebec	I. oboe
_____	10. One of the oldest wind instruments	J. cornet
_____	11. Largest member of the dulcimer family	K. from Bali
_____	12. Smallest of the keyboard instruments	L. maracas

CREATE A CREST

Construct a musical coat of arms. You may create one that represents your favorite type of music, one that shows instruments that you play, or one linked to your cultural heritage. Further personalize your crest with color, your name, and special things about yourself and your connection with this instrument.

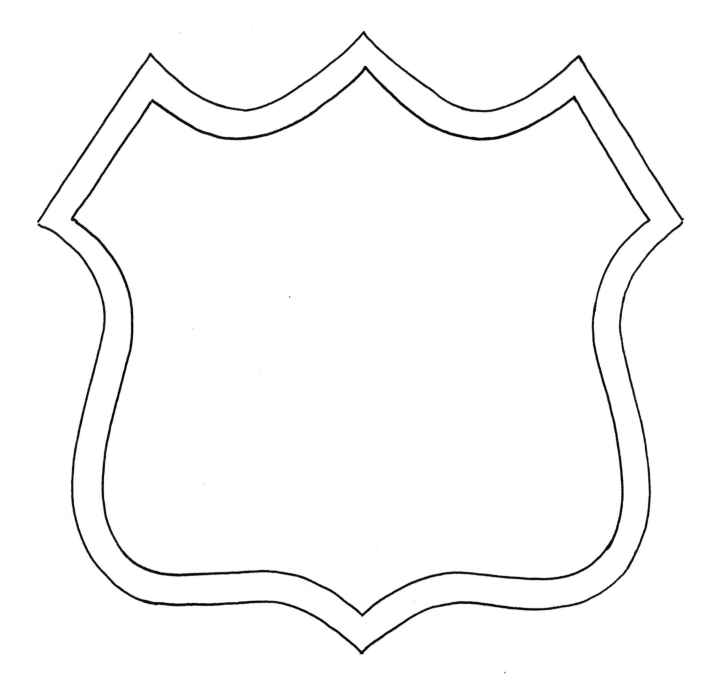

The word *language* comes from the Latin word *lingua* meaning "tongue." Linguistics or philology are names for the science of language study. In today's world, 3,000 tongues are spoken. Some languages are used within a very small area while others are spoken by large numbers of the world's peoples. One hundred languages have a million or more speakers. Nearly 20 languages have 50 million users. Seven hundred different languages can be found in New Guinea. India recognizes 14 official tongues among the many languages heard in that Asian nation.

The Indo-European family of languages is among the most important branches on the world's language tree.

From time to time efforts have been made to create a common world language. *Interlingua* and *esperanto* are two such examples. No such language has achieved lasting popularity, however.

Most people learn their language of origin without thinking about it. Some young children have learned a foreign language (in addition to their own) as early as ages five or six. Foreign language study enables a person to better understand other ways of life and to gain knowledge of cultural customs.

To know a culture's language is to know how the people communicate orally and in written form. These words then become the culture's historical record, a vehicle of entertainment, a mode of communication, and a link to other languages in the world.

Traditionally, people in India are known by the language they speak. For example, Punjabi is spoken by those folks living in the Punjab and Bengali by those people in Bangladesh. Where possible, state lines in the country of India have been drawn according to the language groupings. Difficulties have arisen in those places where languages blend and overlap.

Some sources say the total number of languages and dialects used in India today is between 200 and 250! Hindi, one of the Indo-European languages, is the official language in India.

The greatest disagreement exists between northern India and southern India. The Indo-Aryan language of the north was probably introduced by the Aryans. It is closely related to Sanskrit.

The Dravidian family of languages is most likely to be heard in the south of India. The people who use these tongues resist Hindi being totally official. These people favor English as the official language because it is spoken by literate Indians.

Here is a rough breakdown of the languages spoken in India and the percentage of people who use each one.

Hindi	30%	Urdu	5%	Assamese	2%
Telegu	9%	Gujerati	5%	Oriya	1%
Bengali	8%	Kannada	4%	Kashmiri	1%
Marathi	8%	Malayalam	4%	Other	13%
Tamil	7%	Punjabi	3%		

Further confusion results with languages that are spoken the same but written differently. An example is Urdu written in Arabic script and Hindi written in Devanagri script. They have no common elements, yet they are spoken similarly.

A few words in English that have roots in the language of India include *punch, thug, pariah, shampoo, bungalow,* and *dungarees.*

CONNECT 1: Create charts, flashcards, puzzles, and games to help students learn the languages. Pictures cut from magazines placed on these learning devices can serve as visual aids.

CONNECT 2: Write simple conversational plays in which the limited lessons can be practiced. If students become quite interested, secure a more detailed language book to help them. (Most any book store has or can secure conversational helps for countries all around the world.) Invite someone from your community to come in to serve as a mentor to a group of students who become interested in an in-depth study of a particular language.

CONNECT 3: After two or more language lessons from different countries, ask a group of students to begin a chart series or Venn diagrams to show interrelationships among the tongues.

CONNECT 4: Have the class draw a language tree on a piece of butcher paper. On the branches they can write the names of the languages they have studied.

CONNECT 5: Arrange for students who are especially interested in languages to visit a language class in session. High schools or colleges nearby may prepare special events for visitors or may volunteer to come to your class for sharing.

CONNECT 6: With help from the class, create a game show such as *Jeopardy* or *Wheel of Fortune* where language can be practiced. Emphasize spelling, pronunciation, and use of phrases as you set the rules and guidelines for the game.

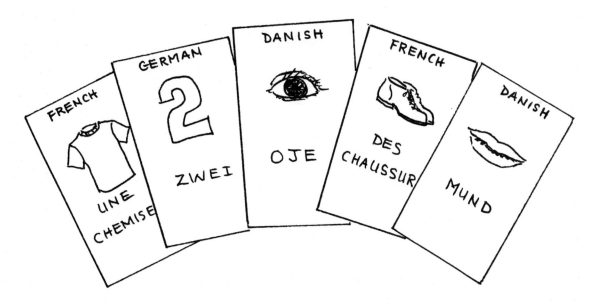

SPEAKING GERMAN

On the West Germanic branch of the language tree are found three closely related tongues—German, Dutch, and English. English and German began to grow apart when the Normans brought many non-Germanic words to England in 1066.

Outside its homeland, German is spoken in Austria and Switzerland. Many older people in eastern European nations have speech rooted in German. Dialects, however, vary.

German is much more phonetic than English and it does not have silent letters. All nouns have capital letters. The gender assigned to the nouns is either masculine, feminine, or neuter, which can be confusing. Stress is "straightforward" with the first syllable usually receiving the accent.

Rhine River

CULTURAL CONNECTIONS

Phrase	See	Say (Emphasize all capitalized syllables)

CONNECT 1:

	Polite phrases	
Hello	Guten Tag	GHU ten TAAK
Good-bye	Auf Wiedersehen	OWF VEE dehr zayn
Yes/No	Ja/Nein	yaa/nain
Please	Bitte	BI teh
Thank you	Danke	DAHNG keh
Good morning	Guten Morgan	GHU tehn MOR ghehn
Good night	Guten Nacht	GHU tehn nahkht
Where are you from?	Woher Kommen Sie?	voh HAYR KO mehn zee?
How old are you	Wie alt sind Sie?	vee ALT zint zee?

CONNECT 2:

	Foreign lands	
I am from	Ich komme aus ___	ikh KO meh ows___
Australia	Australien	pw STRAA li yehn
Canada	Kanada	KAH nah dah
England	England	EHNG lahnt
Germany	Deutschland	DOYCH lahnt
Ireland	Irland	IR lahnt
New Zealand	Neuseeland	noy ZAY lahnt
Scotland	Schottland	SHOT lahnt
Switzerland	der Schweiz	dayhr Shvaits
the United States	den Vereinigten Staaten	dayn fay RAI nikh ten SHTAA teh
Wales	Wales	wailz

CONNECT 3:

	Colors	
blue	schwarz	shvahrts
black	blau	blowh
brown	braun	brown
green	grun	ghrun
orange	orange	OR zheh
pink	rosa	ROH zah
purple	lila	LEE lah
red	rot	roht
white	weiss	vais
yellow	gelb	ghelp

CONNECT 4:

	Numbers	
1	eins	ains
2	zwei (zwo)	tsvai (tsvoh on the telephone)
3	drei	drai
4	vier	feer
5	funf	funf
6	sechs	zehkhs
7	sieben	ZEE ben
8	ach	ahkht
9	neun	noyn
10	zehn	sayn

Many people use the term *Dutch* to refer to the language spoken by residents of the Netherlands and *Flemish* as the tongue of those people in northern Belgium (southern Belgians speak French), but actually Dutch and Flemish are the same.

In United States history, *Dutch* referred to a large number of German immigrants, the Pennsylvania Dutch. The word was a misspoken form of *Deutsch,* meaning German. The people of Holland prefer not to be confused with the Germans, and rightly so, because their languages are as different as Italian and Spanish.

The Afrikaans language of southern Africa is an offshoot of Netherlandic. A few people in former Dutch colonies—Indonesia, the Caribbean, and Surinam—still cling to this tongue.

Netherlandic, too, uses masculine, feminine, and neuter genders for nouns. Flemish tends to be a bit more formal than Dutch. The education and media communities all use General Cultured Netherlandic.

Phrase	See	Say (Emphasize all capitalized syllables)

CONNECT 1:

	Polite greetings	
Hello	Hallo	hal LOH
Good-bye	Dag	Dahkh
Yes/No	Ja/Nee	yaa/nay
Please	Alstublieft	ahls tu BLEEFT
Thank you	Dank U	dahnk u
Good morning	Goede morgen	knoo der MOR khern
Good night	Goede avond	knoo der AA vont

CONNECT 2:

	Occupations	
What work do you do?	Wat doet U?	waht DOOT u?
I am a/an ___	Ik ben een ___	ik behn ern ___
	(male/female)	
student	student/students	stu DEHNT/stu D EHNT er
teacher	leraar/lerares	LEAR aar/lear aar EHS
writer	schrijver/schrijfster	SKHREY ver/SKHREYF ster
lawyer	advocaat/advocate	aht voh KAAT/aht voh KAAT er
doctor	dokter	DOK ter
nurse	verpleger/verpleegster	ver PLAYKH er/ver PLAYKH ster
mechanic	monteur	mon TER
waiter	ober	OH ber
artist	kunstenaar	KERN ster naar
business person	zakenman/zakenvrouw	ZAA kern mahn/ZAA kern vrow
farmer	boer	booer

CONNECT 3:

	Numbers	
1	een	ayn
2	twee	tway
3	drie	dree
4	vier	veer
5	vijf	veyf
6	zes	zehs
7	zeven	ZAY vern
8	acht	ahkht
9	negen	NAY ghen
10	tien	teen

CONNECT 4:

	Colors	
black	zwart	zvahrt
blue	blauw	blow
brown	bruin	brern
green	groen	khroon
pink	rose	RO ser
red	rood	roht
white	wit	vit
yellow	geel	khayl

French is one of the Romance languages. It began to rise as a distinct language in the 800s A.D. Some 750 years later it was declared by Francis I as the compulsory language for French official documents.

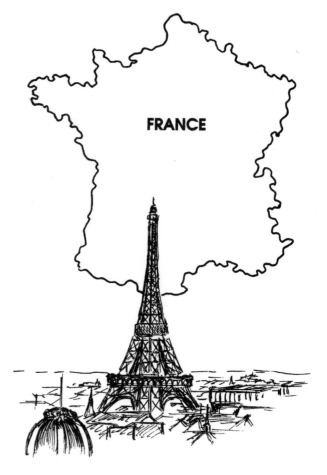

FRANCE

During the sixteenth and seventeenth centuries movements occurred to enrich, then purify, French. Today 90 million of the world's people speak French; 54 million of that number live in France. It is also an official language in Luxembourg, Belgium, and Switzerland. Outside Europe, the largest numbers of people speaking this language can be found in Quebec (Canada), Maine, Louisiana, Africa, the Pacific Islands, and Indochina.

All nouns in French are either masculine or feminine. The adjective that precedes the noun gives the clue. Stress on French syllables is much weaker than English and different parts of each word should be stressed equally.

Phrase	See	Say
CONNECT 1:	**Polite greetings**	
Hello	Bonjour	bo-zhoor
Good-bye	Au revoir	oh rer vwahr
Yes/No	Oui/Non	wee/no
Excuse me	Excusez-moi	ehk sku zei mwah
Please	S'il vous plaît	seel voo plei
Thank you	Merci	mehr see
Good morning	Bonjour	bo-zhoor
Good night	Bonsoir	bo-swahr
CONNECT 2:	**Meals**	
Breakfast	le petit dejeuner	ler per tee dei zher nei
Lunch	le dejeuner	ler dei zher nei
Dinner	le diner	ler dee nei
CONNECT 3:	**Clothing**	
Shirt	une chemise	un sher meez
Trousers	un pantalon	e pa tah lo
Sweater	un pullover	e pu lo verr
Skirt	une jupe	un zhup
Coat	un manteau	e ma toh
Shoes	des chaussures	de shah sur
CONNECT 4:	**Colors**	
black	noir	nwahr
blue	bleu	bler
brown	brun	bre
green	vert	vehr
pink	rose	rohz
red	rouge	roozh
white	blanc	bla
yellow	jaune	zhohn
CONNECT 5:	**Days of the Week**	
Monday	lundi	le dee
Tuesday	mardi	mahr dee
Wednesday	mercredi	mehr krer dee
Thursday	jeudi	zher dee
Friday	vendredi	va drer dee
Saturday	samedi	sahm dee
Sunday	dimanche	de mash
CONNECT 6:	**Numbers**	
1	un	eh
2	deux	der
3	trois	twah
4	quatre	kahtr
5	cinq	sek
6	six	sees
7	sept	seht
8	huit	weet
9	neuf	nerf
10	dix	dees

The Russian alphabet, called the Cyrillic alphabet, has 33 letters. Great Russian, as it is sometimes called, is spoken as a first language by approximately 145 million people. In addition, millions more speak Russian as a second language, particularly those peoples in the eastern part of Europe. Russian is one of the five official languages used at the United Nations.

High cultural significance should be given to Russian literature and the same regard must be accorded to the nation's scientific writings.

It is difficult to master Russian, for it has a free accent; the stress may fall on any syllable. Thus, emphasized syllables must be learned as each word is mastered. Some words with identical spellings are distinguished only by how they are spoken.

THE RUSSIAN CYRILLIC ALPHABET

А	Б	В	Г	Д	Е	Ё	Ж
ah	beh	veh	ggeh	deh	yeh	yoh	zheh

З	И	Й	К	Л	М	Н	О
zeh	ee	ee KRAHT koh yeh	kah	el	em	en	oh

П	Р	С	Т	У	Ф	Х	Ц	Ч
peh	er	es	teh	oo	ef	khah	tseh	chah

Ш	Щ	Ъ	Ы	Ь	Э	Ю	Я
shah	shchah	tv YOR dee znahk	yeh REE	m YAH kee znahk	eh oh boh ROHT noh yeh	yoo	yah

Phrase	Pronounce (Emphasize all capitalized syllables)
CONNECT 1:	**Colors**
red	KRAHS nih
blue	SEE nee
black	CHOHR nih
yellow	ZHOHL tih
green	zee LYOH nih
white	BYEH lih
gray	SYEH rih
brown	kah REECH nee vih
CONNECT 2:	**Polite Phrases**
Good morning	DOH bruh yuh DO truh
Good evening	DOH brih VYEH cheer
Good-bye	dah svee DAH nyuh
How are you?	kakh dee LAH
Please	pah ZHAH loo stuh
Thank You	spah SEE buh
You're welcome	NYEH zah shtuh
CONNECT 3:	**Currency**
ruble	roobl
kopek	kah PYEK kuh
CONNECT 4:	**Numbers**
1	ah DEEN
2	dvah
3	tree
4	chee TIH ryeh
5	piaht
6	shehst
7	siehm
8	VOH seem
9	DYEH veet
10	DYEH seet
How old are you?	SKOHL kuh vahm 1 yeht
I am ___ years old.	Mnyeh ___ 1 yeht

The language of the Danes is, as one would expect, closely related to Swedish, Norwegian, Icelandic, and the language of the peoples of the Faroe Islands. They are all from the north Germanic family.

There are many regional Danish dialects and pronunciation varies from island to island. In Copenhagen *Nudansk,* "new Danish," is used and understood anywhere in this small nation.

Danish is not a language spoken widely outside the homeland. Thus most Danes also learn English.

Usually stress is placed on the first syllable or sometimes on just the first letter of the word. Difficulty arises with Danish because Danes do not always pronounce what they write. There are no set rules for how a given letter should be pronounced.

DENMARK

Phrase	See	Say (Emphasize all capitalized syllables) Pronounce dth as these
CONNECT 1:	**Colors**	
black	sort	soRd
blue	bla	bla
brown	brun	broon
green	gron	grern
orange	orange	o RANG she
pink	rosa	roosa
purple	lilla	LI la
red	rod	rerdth
white	hvid	vidth
yellow	gul	gool
CONNECT 2:	**Parts of the Body**	
arm	arm	aam
back	ryg	rergh
ear	ore	er
eye	oje	ye
finger	finger	fenger
foot	fod	foodth
hand	hand	h'n
heart	hjerte	yaR de
leg	ben	behn
mouth	mund	man
skin	hud	hudth
teeth	taender	tehn
CONNECT 3:	**Polite Greetings**	
Hello	Hallo	haa-lo
Good-bye	Farvel	faar-VEL
Yes/No	Ja/Nej	ya/naay
Please	Majegbede	ma yai bede
Thank you	Tak	taagh
Good morning	God morgen	gho MOR on
Good night	Godnat	gho NAD
CONNECT 4:	**Family**	
brother	bror	broR
sister	soster	ser dth
mother	moder	moodthl
father	far	faa
grandfather	bestefader	behsde fadthl
grandmother	bestemoder	behsde moodthl
family	familie	fa MILYE

Romance languages are those found on the language tree that have roots in Latin, the language of the Romans. Spanish is the most widely spoken of all these tongues. Roman soldiers and merchants brought the base for present-day Spanish to the Iberian peninsula in the period from the third to first centuries B.C. Previous to that, Celtic and Iberian languages had been spoken in this part of Europe. The Arab, Berber, and Moorish influences were felt in the first few centuries A.D., but as Christians returned from northern Spain to southern parts of the peninsula, so did the Spanish that was based on Latin.

With the voyages to America by Christopher Columbus, Spanish language influences were transported to the New World. *Patato, tomate,* and *cacao* are a few examples of the original forms of words we use today that were Spanish imports.

Today's Spanish is more specifically Castilian, one of the three main dialects. Basque is spoken in the north in the region among the Pyrenees Mountains, but little is known of its beginnings. It is of non-Latin origin. A second Romance language, Portuguese, is also heard on the Iberian peninsula.

Pronouncing Spanish is not difficult. It has many sounds which are similar to English. Consistency is found between spelling and pronunciation.

CULTURAL CONNECTIONS

Phrase	See	Say (Emphasize all capitalized syllables)

CONNECT 1:   **Polite Phrases**

Phrase	See	Say
Hello	Hola!	o-lah
Good-bye	Adios!	ah-THios
Yes/no	Si/No	si/no
Please	Por favor	por fah BOR
Thank you	Gracias	GRAH thiahs
Good morning	Buenas dias	BWE nos THI ahs
Good night	Buenas noches	BHE nahs NO ches
How are you?	Como esta?	ko mo es TAH?
Do you speak English?	Habla Ingles?	AH blah in GLES

CONNECT 2:   **Days of the Week**

Phrase	See	Say
Monday	lunes	LOO nes
Tuesday	martes	MAHR tes
Wednesday	miercoles	MIER ko les
Thursday	jueves	HWE bes
Friday	viernes	BIER nes
Saturday	sabado	SAH bah tho
Sunday	domingo	do MIN go

CONNECT 3:   **Months of the Year**

Phrase	See	Say
January	Enero	e NE ro
February	Febrero	fe BRE ro
March	Marzo	MAHR tho
April	Abril	ah BRIL
May	Mayo	Mahy o
June	Junio	HOO nio
July	Julio	HOO lio
August	Agosto	ah GOS to
September	Setiembre	se TIEM bre
October	Octubre	ok TU bre
November	Noviembre	no BIEM bre
December	Diciembre	di THIEM bre

CONNECT 4:   **Numbers**

Phrase	See	Say
1	uno	OO no
2	dos	dos
3	tres	tres
4	cuatro	KWAH tro
5	cinco	THIN ko
6	seis	seis
7	siete	SIE te
8	ocho	O cho
9	nueve	NWE be
10	diez	dieth

CONNECT 5:   **Weather**

Phrase	See	Say
What is the weather today?	Como esta el tiempo?	ko mo es TAH el TIEM po?
It's hot/cold.	Es calor/frio.	es kah/LOR/FRI o

PROUDLY FLY THE FLAG

As you compare the languages among the nations in this section you can see vast differences. Yet surprisingly there are common features, too. The same is true of the flags that represent those countries. Use the organizer below to recreate the symbols and colors of the flags from each country.

Browse through your social studies textbook or another reference source to find the nickname of the country and write it near the flag. Then on a separate sheet of paper, write your personal opinion about why you think the nation's nickname is suitable. If you feel another is more appropriate, write it instead.

FS-10150 Cultural Connections

DANISH DIAGRAM

To review the parts of the body in Danish, use the words below to label the person. Write the word correctly as you place it on or near the location.

OJE   RYG   HUD   TAENDER   FOD   MUND   ARM
FINGER   BEN   ORE   HAND   HJERTE

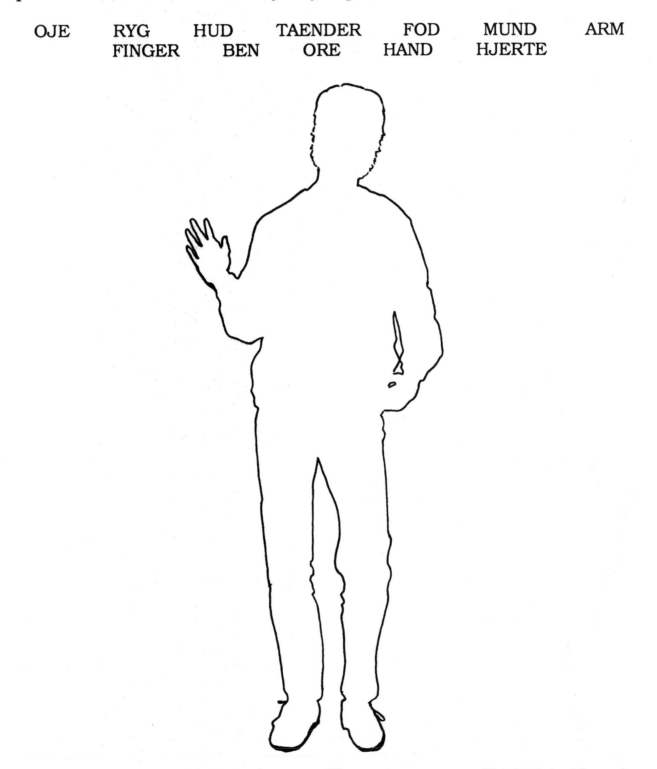

TRANSLATOR NEEDED

As you travel around Europe, you soon become aware of all the languages spoken by peoples there. Below are the official names of those nations as they are spelled in their country. Translate those names. Write the English form in column two. Following that English form, write the word we would use to describe the music, clothing, or food. These will all be proper adjectives.

Example: Republika Bulgaria   Bulgaria   Bulgarian (food)

OFFICIAL NAME	TRANSLATION TO ENGLISH	ADJECTIVE FORM
1. Republick Osterreich		
2. Kongeriget Danmark		
3. Estado Espanol		
4. Schweiz		
5. Eire		
6. Repubblica Italiana		
7. Kongeriket Norge		
8. Konungariket Sverige		
9. Republique Francaise		
10. Royaume de Belgique		

Rudine Sims Bishop says, "Each time we read a good piece of literature we are changed by the experience; we see the world in a new way. It is this capacity to change us, to change our perspective on the world that makes literature a vehicle for understanding cultures and experiences different from our own. Teachers who incorporate literature from various cultures into the classroom can contribute to making tomorrow's world more humane and considerate."

Among the easiest literature selections to incorporate and integrate with other curricular components are examples of folklore. These include legends, fairy tales, myths, riddles, and proverbs. Folk tales come to us through oral tradition. Folk tales include origin stories, stories with repetition that build upon a simple idea, tall tales, and stories with morals.

The story of *Cinderella* is the most loved and most famous folk tale in the world. The Chinese have a version that dates to the ninth century. Cultures in Europe have as many as 500 versions of *Cinderella*. Every culture in the world has its form of the well-known story.

Fairy tales are more polished and sophisticated than folk tales. The latter are short and simple. Fairy tales collected by the Grimm Brothers were known as household tales or *marchen*.

Old books, new printings, and prepared collections are all readily available for teachers to share with students. Perhaps one of the best sources, for a variety of reasons, is the student's own personal library, no matter how small. Do not overlook "little libraries" when searching for examples to share.

To know the literature of a culture is to know its people, their entertainment and values, their hopes and dreams.

ABOUT THE AUTHOR:

The story of Esther Hautzig's life from ages 10–15 is told in her book *Endless Steppe.* The family was routed from their home in Vilna, Poland, and packed into cattle cars for the long train ride to Siberia. Their suffering and triumphs are seen on the pages of *Endless Steppe.*

Following their release from exile, the Rudomin family spent several months in Lodz, Poland. From there they traveled to Stockholm. Stockholm was a stopover on their way to the United States.

It was on the ship to America that Esther met a concert pianist. He was to become her husband. In the United States Esther settled in New York where she completed her high school and college educations. Her career included publication and promotion of books for children.

It was after a visit to Rubtsovsk that Adlai E. Stevenson, American statesman, wrote articles about this Russian city. Esther Rudomin Hautzig read those articles and contacted Mr. Stevenson to explain her connection to this place. In his reply to her, Stevenson suggested she share her story of life on the Siberian steppe during the war. *Endless Steppe* was the result.

ABOUT THE STORY:

From June, 1941, until March, 1946, Esther Rudomin lived in the Siberian wilderness with members of her family. They had come from Vilna, Poland, to the vast wasteland by cattle car. They were Polish Jews forced into exile. Their crime? They were capitalists.

After weeks of cramped quarters in the cattle cars, Esther's parents and grandmother arrived in the village of Rubtsovsk. Esther describes it as "a frontier village built around a large open square...as if the muddy paths were laid out for tick-tack-toe."

From the village the family was sent to a gypsum mine on the treeless steppe. Here they endured endless hardships and deprivation.

Before long, Tata (papa) was sent to the front lines of the war to work in a labor brigade. Among the family's sufferings Esther finds a few bright spots—school, small jobs knitting and crocheting, the library and books, friends, and the beauty of the land itself.

Esther longed for her beloved past, for her comfortable home, for enough to eat, for family members, for cherished possessions. When the family was released at the end of the war, they hoped against hope that their old home in Vilna had survived and they would be able to return. This was not the case and as the Rudomin family members made way to Lodz, Poland, they went with nothing but memories of their former life.

CULTURAL CONNECTIONS

CONNECT 1: Have a group of students create a time line that recounts important world events before and after World War II. From this quick glance at history the class can more easily see where the story of Esther and her family fits into the large scene.

CONNECT 2: In a class discussion compare and contrast the lives of Polish Jews who were sent into exile with those who were sent to concentration camps in Poland.

CONNECT 3: Have each student locate several of Esther's descriptions of the beauty of the endless steppe and select one that is particularly appealing. Then the students can sketch, draw, and color these scenes as pictured through Mrs. Hautzig's words.

CONNECT 4: Secure copies of a map of the former Soviet Union. Locate and mark the region of Siberia. Within its borders, have students jot down notable information about the setting of *Endless Steppe*. Does the research source compare favorably with Esther Hautzig's?

CONNECT 5: Investigate some of the literary selections and/or authors that Esther encountered in her schooling. Share a favorite with the class.

CONNECT 6: Discuss capitalism, the crime for which the Rudomins were sent into exile.

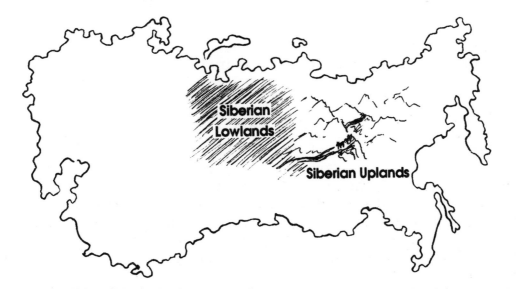

Over 200 years ago in the German principality of Hesse in the city of Kassel there lived two brothers. Jakob Ludwig Grimm, reclusive, stern-faced, crotchety, and slight of build, preferred to be seated at his desk writing with a quill pen. Wilhelm Karl Grimm, his younger brother, witty, lively, high-spirited, and lanky, was often seen under a tree scribbling as someone retold a story for him.

Traveling and collecting, collecting and traveling were not especially easy for the Grimms. From shepherds, old soldiers, innkeepers, and the old spinning women, the Grimms and their friends collected the stories. The collection grew into unwieldy stacks. A friend finally drove the brothers to publish the first volume. It was a group of 86 stories, available in time for Christmas, 1812. It was entitled, *Nursery and Household Tales.* Critics were aghast at once, saying that many of the tales were unsuitable for children, labeling them "shocking" and "coarse." Despite this, the collection sold 900 copies, second only to the Bible, and became the most widely read book in Germany.

The second edition of 70 stories appeared in 1819 with engravings by their brother, Ludwig Emil. Over the years 17 more editions were published.

A German grammar was compiled by Jakob in 1819. A dictionary in German was begun a few years later but was not completed by the brothers.

German history, nature, the supernatural, fantasy, and mythology all appear in these fairy tales. Many of the stories have similarities to stories from cultures half a world away. These are perhaps tales that were told by travelers. They illustrate commonalities among the world's peoples.

The Grimms were not happy when their stories were called children's literature. They intended their books for adults as well as young people. They felt that people of all ages share similar dreams, desires, and emotions. Their harvest of folk tales is the best evidence of this truth.

REPRESENTATIVE SAMPLES:

"The Pied Piper"- The mysterious stranger tricked by the town council returns the favor with the help of his magic flute.

"Bremen Town Musicians"- Four animals running away from injustices work together to defeat a band of robbers.

"Cinderella"- Mistreated by her stepmother and stepsisters, Cinderella is rewarded by her fairy godmother.

"Snow White"- The recipient of a spell, Snow White is punished because of her beauty.

"Rumpelstiltskin"- Desperate to save her infant child the new queen overcomes the trickery of the little man.

"Little Red Riding Hood"- Danger awaits the little girl who is traveling through the woods on the way to Grandma's.

"The Fisherman and His Wife"- The fisherman's wife asks for too much from the magic flounder, then loses everything.

"Little Thumb"- After many trials and tribulations the tiny son is happily returned to his family.

"The Shoemaker and the Elves"- Kindness is rewarded and the couple have enough money to last them their lifetimes.

"The Golden Bird"- There are three sons, two of whom are disloyal; the youngest marries the beautiful princess.

"The Golden Goose"- The third silly son shares with the gray old man and is rewarded with a goose with feathers of gold.

"The Brave Little Tailor"- Dangerous fellows the tailor meets misunderstand his waist-belt motto, "Seven at one stroke."

"Rapunzel"- A girl (whose name is "lettuce" in German) and her prince are mistreated by the witch but triumph in the end.

CONNECT 1: Appoint a group of students to create a listing of 10–15 familiar tales collected by the Grimm brothers. (There are 215 altogether!) Make copies of the list in the form of a questionnaire. Have the group poll their classmates, asking them to mark the stories with which they are familiar and to star their favorite. Then the committee can collect the forms, graph the choices, and share the information and the winning story with the class. Close with a discussion of why this folktale received the most votes.

CONNECT 2: Using an atlas, find the area of Hesse and the town of Kassel in Germany. Mark a 100-mile radius from Kassel in many directions. See what other familiar cities, rivers, mountains, and other features students can find near Kassel. No doubt these are among the places visited by the Grimm Brothers. Are there changes within the radius that Jakob and Wilhelm would not recognize?

CONNECT 3: Make arrangements to visit a retirement home in your community. Ask an activities director there to locate older folks who would be willing to tell you a favorite story they recall from childhood. On the day you visit, take along a tape recorder to record the story. Share the taped tales with the class when you return to school. Discuss and compare these oral stories with Grimm Brothers samples or with stories you are likely to read today. Are there more similarities or differences?

CONNECT 4: Assign students to select and update one of the Grimm Brothers stories. They can change the speech, perhaps the setting, and update the clothing, anything to bring this old story into present times. They can illustrate their versions if they wish.

CONNECT 5: Ask each student to create an entirely new tale by taking single characters from any number of Grimm Brothers stories. For instance a class member could write a new story with these characters: the Pied Piper, Cinderella's fairy godmother, a dwarf from *Snow White*, Rumpelstiltskin, and the rooster from "Bremen Town Musicians."

Each student can tell his/her original story with puppets or share it by reading aloud.

THE BIG WAVE

ABOUT THE AUTHOR:

Pearl Sydenstricker Buck was born in Hillsboro, West Virginia, in 1892. At an early age her missionary parents took her to China. Her mother taught Pearl that "beauty lies in words and what words will say."

JAPAN

Pearl Buck's novel *The Good Earth,* written in 1931, won a Pulitzer Prize. The success of the story about China eventually led to a Nobel Prize in Literature in 1938.

The Big Wave was written in 1948. Buck had returned to America and was working as an editor in New York. In 1951 she was one of two women elected to the American Academy of Arts and Letters, a group of 50 life members.

Much of her writing was done in the 1940s and 1950s. In addition to works about China, Buck wrote about Russia, Japan, and Germany. It was her goal to bring distant parts of the globe together through her stories. She died in 1973.

ABOUT THE STORY:

Kino is the son of a Japanese farmer whose family lives on the mountainside. Jiya's family is made up of fishermen who reside in the village near the ocean. The young boys sometimes discuss whether the sea is a beautiful thing or an enemy. Then comes the day when sea and earth and sky work against man and a tidal wave destroys the village on the beach.

Jiya's family is swept away and Jiya vacillates between accepting life's pain and giving up.

Old Gentleman offers to take Jiya into the castle to become his son. His generous gesture prompts Kino and Jiya to visit the old man's luxurious home.

The friendship between Kino and Jiya grows stronger as they support one another following the tragedy. They both find happiness in the different life styles they choose living with the earth and the sea.

CULTURAL CONNECTIONS

CONNECT 1: Have each student print a favorite saying or motto on a scroll and design and decorate the scroll to resemble Japanese style. Each person can share his/her scroll with the class and, as Old Gentleman did, hang it where it can be seen each day.

CONNECT 2: Explain how a tidal wave differs from a hurricane and from a tornado. Lead a class discussion about the warning signs that people in Japan would recognize before a tidal wave approaches.

CONNECT 3: Kino's father explains his philosophy of living with danger and of handling fear. Read aloud to the class the situation in which he talks about enjoying life and not fearing death. This is the way of a good Japanese. Ask students how they feel about this philosophy. Discuss its pros and cons.

CONNECT 4: Locate copies of Elizabeth Coatsworth's Newbery Medal book, *Cat Who Went to Heaven.* Offer extra credit to readers who are willing to read this story and compare Japanese traditions as portrayed by Elizabeth Coatsworth and Pearl Buck.

CONNECT 5: Discuss with students the evidence that points to the likelihood that this sort of natural occurrence will repeat itself in this part of the world.

IT IS BETTER TO LIGHT ONE SMALL CANDLE THAN TO CURSE THE DARKNESS

CONFUCIUS

ABOUT THE AUTHOR:

Johanna Spyri lived from 1827 until 1901. Her entire life was spent in a small village near Zurich, Switzerland. Her father, Dr. Heusser, was the local physician. Her early school life was, like Heidi's, not particularly successful. Johanna eventually left her village school to study with the local pastor. Later in her life, she married Zurich's town clerk, Bernhard Spyri. They had one son.

SWITZERLAND

Johanna loved the Swiss countryside—the animals, mountains, plants, and flowers. *Heidi* is nearly an autobiography. Mrs. Spyri wrote the book to raise money for a war relief fund. This book, as well as the many that followed it, deals with the pleasures of life in a Swiss mountain village.

ABOUT THE STORY:

Orphaned at age one, Heidi is now five. Aunt Dete has an opportunity for a better job in Frankfurt and has decided Heidi should go to the mountain to live with Heidi's grandfather. The old man is called Alm Uncle, for he resides on Alm Mountain in the Swiss Alps. Many fear him because of his bad temperament and his decision to move away from God and man.

Heidi loves her new home, her room in the loft, the goatherd, Peter, and his goats, the beauty of the mountainside, and her grandfather. Peter's mother and his blind grandmother become Heidi's good friends.

When Heidi turns eight, Aunt Dete returns to the mountain to take the child to Frankfurt. Relatives of the family Dete works for have an invalid daughter, Klara, who needs a companion. Aunt Dete feels this is also a good arrangement for her niece, a chance to polish the rough edges.

In Klara's home Heidi learns to read as she and Klara become friends. Yet Heidi is terribly lonely for the mountain and for her grandfather.

At last Heidi returns to her mountain home, where Klara eventually visits. The heartwarming connections among the mountain folks and the family from Frankfurt create a happy ending to this picture of life styles in the Swiss mountain villages 100 years ago.

CONNECT 1: Discuss with the class what sent Uncle to the top of Alm Mountain. Why would such a location be suitable for someone who wished to live away from other villages?

CONNECT 2: Divide the class into small groups and have each create a booklet of sketches showing examples of the flora and fauna found in an Alpine ecosystem. They can add color if they wish or create blackline drawings to be painted or colored by other members of the class.

CONNECT 3: Have these same groups investigate the breeds of goats raised in places like Swiss villages. Which breeds are specially bred to produce milk for cheese?

Going one step further, have students research and report on the steps required to produce cheese from goat's milk.

CONNECT 4: Using maps of Switzerland and Germany, have the class decide upon a likely route Aunt Dete may have taken going from Dorfli to her new position in Frankfurt.

CONNECT 5: With the class, make a listing of the names given to the goats in Peter's herd. Ask students to explain why the creatures may have gotten those names.

Ask students to think of names of pets they have had. Discuss why we use certain names for pets. Brainstorm reasons for the types of names we give to animals we know and love.

CONNECT 6: Have the class help you create a diorama depicting what Heidi saw the first time she entered Grandfather's alpine hut.

EGYPT

ABOUT THE AUTHOR:

Zilpha Keatley Snyder was born in California in 1927. She is a wife and mother and spent nearly a decade as a public school teacher. The six main characters in *The Egypt Game* are based on real young people who were in her class in Berkeley, California. Teaching proved to be an asset to Mrs. Snyder as a writer. Students were an inspiration and also taught her to speak their language.

Her desire to write began in her childhood. She grew up during the depression and World War II. Animals and books filled her life. The library near her home "was an inexhaustible storehouse of adventure and excitement" to her. She believes she read a book a day during her childhood. When she was eight, Zilpha discovered that books were written by ordinary people and she decided then that that was the kind of person she wanted to be.

The following books were creations by Mrs. Snyder for which she received honors from various sources: *The Egypt Game, The Changeling, The Headless Cupid,* and *The Witches of Worm.* They are among nearly two dozen books she has written.

ABOUT THE STORY:

When April arrives to live with her paternal grandmother, she is certain the stay will be a short one. Her show business mother will find work soon and then she will return home to Hollywood.

The Casa Rosada, the apartment house where her grandmother lives, is an aging structure of Spanish architecture known by the residents as "the petrified birth-day cake." Within its walls, lonely April finds things she has lacked in her life, friendship and love.

Caroline, April's grandmother, introduces April to the Ross family. Eleven-year-old Melanie Ross and her four-year-old brother Marshall become April's close companions. The girls discover a common interest—ancient Egypt. It becomes a game and eventually leads to the deserted storage area in the professor's backyard.

When Elizabeth and two boys from school join the group, the Egypt gang is complete. Spare time is spent on costumes, codes, and ceremonies. A mixture of mystery, magic, and murder soon add new dimensions to the game. This delightful tale reveals how an ancient people's traditions and history can touch the lives of young people in modern times.

Zilpha Keatley Snyder's Newbery Honor Book is particularly good when shared orally by the teacher.

CONNECT 1: Have the class create a desk-top model of what the storage yard looked like when the gang first discovered it. As the story proceeds they can make the same changes in this model that the Egypt gang makes to the actual setting.

CONNECT 2: Assign cooperative-learning groups to create an original magazine family like April and Melanie did. They can mount the cutouts on tagboard for stability and orally present a story about the family to other groups in the room.

CONNECT 3: Have each student make an ongoing list of authentic Egypt information as revealed in the story, including words, names, and traditions that are actually part of ancient Egyptian culture.

CONNECT 4: Discuss with the class the friendships among the varied members of the Egypt gang. Note the diversity in age and race.

CONNECT 5: Locate an actual set of hieroglyphics. Have each student write a message using this ancient form to give an opinion of this story. Students can exchange secret messages with friends to decipher.

CONNECT 6: Ask members of the class to predict events that could be included in a sequel to this story, a tale of Gypsies as suggested on the last page of *The Egypt Game*.

CALL IT COURAGE

ABOUT THE AUTHOR:

Armstrong Sperry was an American author and illustrator born in 1897 in New Haven, Connecticut. He studied art at the Yale Art School and also in New York City.

He became interested in the sea early in his life. He sat time after time listening to his great-grandfather tell of his adventures as a sea captain in the South Seas. The elder man had delightful yarns to share with his great-grandson.

Call It Courage was written after Sperry had spent two years in the South Pacific. The story won the Newbery Medal in 1941.

The Newbery Medal is a prize created by Frederic Melcher, American publisher and editor. It is given each year to an author whose story is chosen as the greatest contribution to literature for children in America. Mr. Melcher named the medal for John Newbery, England's first publisher of children's books.

ABOUT THE STORY:

Mafatu, son of the chief, witnesses the death of his mother at sea. Named Stout Heart by his father, Mafatu is continually troubled by the tragedy and cannot overcome his fear of the sea. Labeled a coward by his peers and scorned by the villagers, Mafatu takes Uri, the yellow dog, and sails out into the mysterious ocean.

His travels are a constant battle between Moana, the sea god who seeks to claim him, and Maui, god of the fishermen, who protects him.

Recalling adventures of his Grandfather Ruau, Mafatu resolves to perform tasks that will earn him respect when he returns to his people. Even pursuit by savages does not prevent him from achieving his goals and proving himself and his courage to the villagers.

CONNECT 1: Have students write an opinion statement in which they state whether they agree or disagree that Mafatu does have to prove his courage to his family and the other villagers.

CONNECT 2: The class can make a directory of the proper nouns the author uses to add "flavor" to the story of life in the Pacific Islands.

CONNECT 3: Then they can illustrate these specialized vocabulary words used by Armstrong Sperry in *Call It Courage*. Some examples are: *outrigger, breadfruit, guava, mango, coconuts, sea urchins, albatross, and frigate bird.*

CONNECT 4: Have a student volunteer use colored pencils to outline on a map of the South Pacific, the regions known as Polynesia, Micronesia, and Melanesia.

CONNECT 5: Using a Venn diagram, have students compare and contrast Chapter 4 of Armstrong Sperry's story with Karana's survival in *Island of the Blue Dolphins.*

CONNECT 6: In a class discussion evaluate the way Mafatu and his people so expertly used the natural materials at hand in their daily living.

HANS BRINKER, OR, THE SILVER SKATES

ABOUT THE AUTHOR:

Mary Mapes Dodge was born in New York City in 1831. Her father encouraged his young daughter in her early attempts at writing.

She married at age 20 and had two children. Her husband died when she was 28. With the children to care for she began a serious career in writing and editing.

Hans Brinker, or, the Silver Skates was produced in 1865. This story was written in a farmhouse in New Jersey and became a children's classic. By working with Dutch immigrants and reading about Holland, Mary Mapes Dodge produced authentic portraits of the canals, windmills, and dykes of Holland, and the Dutch culture in the nineteenth century.

Mrs. Dodge worked on the staff for the publishers of *Hearth and Home.* In 1873 she became editor of the *St. Nicholas Magazine for Boys and Girls.* She held that position for 30 years.

Notable writers who worked with her in an effort to make literature entertaining for boys and girls of this era included Mark Twain, Rudyard Kipling, and Jack London.

ABOUT THE STORY:

As Mary Mapes Dodge tells her story of the Brinker family, it is clear that she is also relating the story of the land and the culture of the people of Holland. Among the threads of the interrelationships of the neighborhood young people and the positions of the village adults, she expertly weaves the geography and traditions of the Dutch. Holiday celebrations, history, and language are as important to the book as the tragedies that have befallen the Brinker and Boekman families.

Hans is 15 and Gretel Brinker is 12 when the story opens. Hard times have befallen them since their father suffered a head injury during efforts to save a flood dyke 10 years earlier. Raf Brinker does not even know his family. He cannot tell them where he hid their family savings.

When Dr. Boekman operates successfully on Raf Brinker, the unusual connection between Raf and the doctor's son is discovered.

Hans and Gretel both participate in the December 20 ice skating race on the arm of the Zuider Zee. In different ways both are winners.

As the book nears its end, Hans becomes a second son to Dr. Boekman. Then in the Conclusion, an epilogue, Mrs. Dodge creates a glimpse into the future of the lives of the main characters and we see what life had in store for them.

CONNECT 1: Have students draw and compare the wooden *Klompen* the Dutch wear with the wooden skates Hans wore in the race.

CONNECT 2: Ask the class to reread Chapter Two, "Holland," and explain why the author set aside a whole chapter to present such a detailed description of the setting for this story. Mrs. Dodge refers to the descriptors as "oddities of Holland." Can the students think of any unique phrases to describe where they live? Have each student write about his/her location in the style of Mary Mapes Dodge.

CONNECT 3: At the end of Chapter 8 a footnote is given to explain the difference between the Dutch mile and our statute mile. Have students convert the distance from Broek to the Hague using this information. How many other different "miles" are there? Then they can locate them on a chart which can be posted in your classroom.

CONNECT 4: In the middle of Chapter 10, the skaters visit the art museum. Locate paintings by Dutch masters and/or other artists named here. Share the photos or reproductions with the class. Are there visual clues here to further tell how Dutch culture is unique?

CONNECT 5: Ask for a volunteer to recount the history of the tulip as described in Chapter 11 and to recall the small contribution artist Judith Leyster made to this chapter of the Dutch nation's floral history.

CONNECT 6: Use the outline map of Holland as a sheet on which students can record the actual place names Mary Mapes Dodge describes in the book. Examples are Amsterdam, Leyden, Haarlen, the Hague, Delft, and Rotterdam. A short phrase could be included to point out significant features of each of these cities.

HOLLAND

FAIRY TALES OF HANS CHRISTIAN ANDERSEN

Denmark's most famous author, Hans Christian Andersen, lived from April 2, 1805, to August 4, 1875. The son of a shoemaker, Andersen lived in the village of Odense (OH den say) on the island of Fyn. The poor family's treasure was a cupboard filled with books above the father's workbench. Both parents read news and told stories to their son, Hans.

When Andersen was 11, his father died, and two years later his mother remarried. He received very little acknowledgment from his stepfather. Hans did not look or act like other children. He was tall and thin and had big feet and a long nose between tiny eyes. His mother longed for him to be a tailor but Hans had earned a reputation as an entertainer. He was often asked into private homes to sing, act, and read poetry.

In 1819 Hans left Odense for Copenhagen. He stumbled through singing, dance, and ballet lessons. He had almost no money and was usually hungry. He entertained children with stories and cuttings made of folded paper.

At age 17, Andersen returned to school. Six years later he finished his studies and began writing. Between projects he traveled. He returned to Odense to visit his mother, who was now in a poorhouse. In 1833 the Danish king gave Hans money to travel in Italy, Switzerland, Germany, and France. Among his contemporaries were Charles Dickens and Franz Liszt.

Hans Christian Andersen's works include travel books, plays, poetry, novels, and autobiographical writings. Andersen's fairy tales, *Smaarting* or trifles as he called them, numbered over 100. These tales do not always end happily and are among the most published works in literary history. Many were intended to be shared with Andersen's adult friends. No matter what audience he wrote for, his stories were based on childhood recollections and were created in his fertile mind.

CONNECT 1: Label an outline map of Denmark's four major islands and ask the class these questions: Which one is called the thumb of the hand of Germany? Approximately how far is it from Odense to Copenhagen? Ask a volunteer to mark two different routes on the map to show how Hans Christian Andersen might have gotten from his hometown to Denmark's capital city.

CONNECT 2: Ask the class to determine what nations Charles Dickens and Franz Liszt are from and then to calculate the distances from Copenhagen to the capitals of the nations these famous contemporaries of Andersen's called home.

CONNECT 3: Locate copies of the stories written by Hans Christian Andersen. Have the class select ones appropriate for young children and make arrangements to recite or read these to younger students in your school.

CONNECT 4: Napoleon, Emperor of France, was a hero to Andersen's father. Napoleon was fighting against Russia at the time the boy was growing up. Denmark helped the French in this war. Assign a small group of students to research some details about Napoleon and the war and then lead a class discussion about how Hans, a boy of 9 or 10, might have reacted to these events in history.

CONNECT 5: Create a t-box. Label the columns with a plus and a minus. Then have students locate and place in the box happenings in Andersen's life that they consider positive and negative events. Which list is longer? Then ask students to consider these questions: Are there times in your life when you feel things are not balanced? What kind of attitude is needed to even out the balance? Did Hans Christian Andersen display this approach to life?

CONNECT 6: Several of Andersen's stories became films. The most recent is *The Little Mermaid.* Ask the class to make a comparison between print and film. Were changes made? Have them explain and point out their evidence.

THINK CRITICALLY

It is unrealistic to assume you will enjoy every book or story that you choose to read or that is assigned to you.

It is equally important for you to be able to identify what you do not like in an author's work.

Choose a book you have read recently, one of the ones in this section or something outside the class. Then complete the form below with your honest opinions.

Title _____

Author _____

Short summary of the story:

_____

_____

_____

_____

_____

Your main criticism of the story:

_____

_____

_____

_____

_____

How you feel the book could be improved:

_____

_____

_____

_____

_____

ETYMOLOGY

Sampling literature from different world settings helps us to see the many connections among languages. Below are words we use from German, French, and Spanish. Complete the lists by adding a few words of your own. (Your spelling book is often a good source.) At the right is a space for interesting extras you discover as you investigate word origins.

NOTES

WORDS FROM GERMANY

cologne

frankfurter

hamburg

_____

_____

WORDS FROM FRENCH

bon voyage

café

hors d'oeuvre

_____

_____

WORDS FROM SPANISH

barbecue

plaza

lariat

_____

_____

Name: _____

Geographers group the many islands of the South Pacific into these three sections: MELANESIA, MICRONESIA, and POLYNESIA. Use a map to correctly place the islands under the three headings.

MELANESIA

_____ _____
_____ _____
_____ _____
_____ _____

MICRONESIA

_____ _____
_____ _____
_____

POLYNESIA

_____ _____
_____ _____
_____ _____
_____ _____
_____ _____
_____ _____

American Samoa
Caroline
Cook
Easter
Ellice
Fiji
Gilbert
Guam
Hawaii
Kermadec
Line
Loyalty
Mariana
Marquesas
Marshall
Midway
New Caledonia
New Hebrides
Papua New Guinea
Phoenix
Pitcairn
Society
Solomon
Tahiti
Tuamotu
Vanuatu
Western Samoa

Challenge: Research to find out if these island groups are independent or protected/governed by another nation.

         FS-10150 Cultural Connections

QUITE A CHARACTER

Character traits are words that describe people's actions, rather than their looks. Think of the characters from *Endless Steppe*. Here are some words that tell how characters in the story lived their lives. Add others in the blanks.

proud   determined   adventurous

patient   brave   caring

loving   courageous   thoughtful

_____   _____   _____

_____   _____   _____

Think back to the people from *Endless Steppe*. Under each name, jot the words from the total list that best describe the people. Be able to justify your selection.

ESTHER   GRANDMOTHER

_____   _____

_____   _____

MR. RUDOMIN   RAISA NIKITOVNA

                                    (the teacher)

_____   _____

_____   _____

MRS. RUDOMIN   SVETLANA

                                  (girl at school)

_____   _____

_____   _____

PREFACE

CHAPTER 6
FOOD

Earth's first peoples were hunters and gatherers. To obtain meat, early man learned to outwit and ensnare deer, elk, sheep, wild boar, hippos, and seals. Fish and birds were also hunted to feed individuals and groups. Early peoples also collected roots, berries, nuts, and seeds. It is estimated that cultivation of crops began about 10,000 years ago. By 3000 B.C., carrots, onions, lettuce, and beans were among the crops being grown.

Sheep and goats were among the first animals to be domesticated, thereby providing a steady supply of meat when wild game was unavailable. By 4000 B.C., cattle were tamed and meat *and* milk were available from a single source.

Further advancements occurred as more sophisticated tools and techniques evolved. Irrigation and selective breeding clearly put man in control in the growing of crops.

Early in history (as now) geography played a major role in what people found, grew, and ate. Location and climate determined, and soils and terrain dictated, what was grown or gathered. Tropical areas provided fresh fruits and vegetables year-round. In cooler areas with short growing seasons, root crops and grains were common. Island and seacoast residents depended on fish from nearby waters.

There are many interesting customs related to the world's peoples and their food. Hindus do not eat beef because cattle are sacred to them. Muslims have fasting during Ramadan, the ninth month of their year. They do not eat from sunrise to sunset. Then the fast is broken by a feast. Orthodox Jews have specific rules for preserving, serving, and storing foods.

Many nations and cultures have traditional dishes. Basic ingredients may be used in many areas but regional seasonings and methods of cooking create distinctive dishes. For some cultures the serving of the food has special meaning. For instance, the Japanese dishes can be as beautiful to look at as they are delicious to eat. The Swedish smorgasbord is a favorite of all who experience it.

Culture and custom determine when people eat. The British add a fourth meal called tea to their regime. Most Americans eat three meals a day but the time of the main meal often varies depending on whether people live in urban or rural areas.

Many people consider France the center of the finest cookery and home of many renowned chefs. But many places around the world have their own particular reputations in cuisine, such as the following:

German bratwurst and cabbage dishes	Japanese tofu and sushi
Italian pasta and sauces	Indian curry
Mexican tortillas and tacos	Mideastern shish kabobs
Chinese stir-fry with rice	Scandinavian breads and fish

Modern transportation and communication have greatly contributed to the world exchange of food and eating habits. From open fires to microwaves, from Australia to America, peoples of the world eat more alike than ever before.

As in other cultural areas, the Romans and Moors made major contributions to the foods produced in Spain. Both early peoples designed efficient irrigation systems to help in watering arid Spanish soils. Later in history when Spanish explorers returned from expeditions abroad, they brought new food stuffs for new Spanish eating styles. Chocolate, vanilla, potatoes, tomatoes, eggplant, and beans were not native to the Iberian peninsula until introduced by explorers.

Shopping for food in Spain is usually a daily task done at the market or special grocers. Large supermarkets are found but are not preferred by most Spanish cooks. The colorful displays of fresh goods in the open-air market are inviting and foods bought there are often more flavorful.

Seafood transported daily to the open-air markets by trucks from the coastal waters include lobster, shrimp, mussels, clams, hake, and squid. Chickens are brought live to these markets, then killed after being purchased. Freshness is guaranteed! Olive oil containers are brought from home and filled at the market. There are numerous kinds and qualities of this oil used regularly by Spanish cooks.

In Spain regional specialities are found, too. Cooking in northwest Spain resembles that of Brittany and Normandy in France. Stews are popular. Fabada stew made with the *fabe*, white bean stew, seafood stew with cornbread, and *empañada*, a cold meat or seafood pie are all favorites.

The Basques in the valley of the Pyrenees are hefty eaters. Family bonds are strong and sharing good food is celebrated among the Basques. Meat, fish, poultry, vegetables, and soups may all be prepared for their special meals.

In northeast Spain, sauces of ham, peppers, garlic, onion, and tomato are specialties. On the east coast, rice and oranges are grown. *Paella*, a stew of rice, vegetables, chicken, and seafood is also enjoyed.

In hot Andalusia in the south, gazpacho–cold, blended vegetable soup–is a treat. Add *sangria*, a fruity punch, and crisply fried fish for a delightful Andalusian meal.

Catalonian style dishes feature fresh fruits in summer, calamari (squid), vegetables, and fresh mushrooms.

Around Madrid and the central Meseta (a high plateau that covers most of Spain), foods from all around Spain can be sampled. Roasted game, in season, adds variety to the dishes eaten on a regular basis.

Spanish meals are:

El Desayuno - Breakfast is typically a small meal of bread and coffee or milk.

La Comida - Dinner is a large meal of from four to six courses which is eaten between 2 p.m. and 4 p.m.

La Cena - Supper is a light meal of soup, salad, cheese, and fruit served about 10:30 or 11:00 p.m.

Try this Spanish dish:

Paella, Spain's National Dish

1. In a wide skillet, cook for 10 minutes 8 oz. of garlic-seasoned sausage. Drain, cool, slice, and set aside.

2. Heat 2 Tbs. of cooking oil or olive oil. Add a 2 ½ lb. chicken, cut into eight serving pieces. Turn the chicken as it browns. Cook for 15 minutes. Remove chicken and set aside.

3. In saucepan heat to boiling 4 cups of chicken broth

4. In wide skillet with the remaining oil, brown 1 onion, cut into wedges and 1 red or green pepper, cut into strips.

5. Preheat oven to 400°.

6. To onion and pepper in the skillet add 2 cups white rice, uncooked, the chicken broth, ½ tsp. oregano, and ¼ tsp. saffron.

7. On top of the rice mixture, arrange chicken pieces, sausage slices, ½ cup canned shrimp, and ½ cup canned clams.

8. Over the top scatter ½ package of frozen peas.

9. Set pan on the bottom of the oven and bake uncovered 25-30 minutes. Never stir paella after it goes into the oven. After cooking, let rest five minutes. Serve from the pan.

CONNECT 1: Make copies of an outline map of Spain and have students draw in regions and products mentioned in the text on the preceding page. Then they can color and label each area to identify it and add one or two well-known metropolitan areas in each region.

CONNECT 2: Have students draw pictures that show a typical market scene in a Spanish city. Encourage them to browse through a Spanish/English dictionary to locate names of fruits and vegetables that might be found in a market and add those names to the drawing.

CONNECT 3: The Spanish enjoy a wide variety of seafood in their diets. Help familiarize students with different types of fish and seafood by creating a Seafood Alphabet book in which class members name and describe products from the sea for each letter.

Geography and climate impact crops and foods in Norway as in other parts of the world. Fish is a mainstay for these Norwegian people who live on the water. Herring, mackerel, and salmon are caught in Norwegian waters. *Torsk* (cod), the most plentiful, is often called "poor man's lobster." Much fish is preserved for winter use. Torsk is often salted and fried, dried in the cool Norwegian air, smoked, or dipped in lye to preserve it. The last process produces *Lutefisk*. Lutefisk is still prepared in the United States by people of Scandinavian heritage.

The Gulf Stream tempers Norway's northern climate and, although the weather remains damp and cool, vegetables such as cabbage, cauliflower, rutabagas, carrots, and potatoes thrive. Berries found in this climate include blueberries, lingonberries, strawberries, and cloudberries. Cloudberries are a type of raspberry, orangish-yellow, that grow in the mountains "near the clouds."

Norwegians are given credit for the origin of the *smorgasbord,* a popular buffet featuring a wide variety of foods.

Norwegian meals are
> *Frokost* - Breakfast in Norway might include rice porridge or oatmeal, cheese and flatbread (rye-crisp).
> *Lunsj* - Lunch is eaten around 12:00 or 1:00 p.m. Sandwiches and soups are common.
> *Middag* - Dinner is the evening meal, a time for families to be together. At this meal, served between 6:30 and 7:00 p.m., meatballs, fish, potatoes, vegetables, and a pudding might be enjoyed.

Afterschool snacks for children or adults are popular in Norway. *Lefse,* a thin potato cake with brown freckles, is tasty plain or buttered and sprinkled with sugar. *Kavring,* wheat rusks, is a crunchy dried bread. Butter or cheese atop a piece of *flatbrod* or rye crisp and fruit make good snacks.

Try this Norwegian recipe:

Flatbread

Combine in a bowl:
    1 ⅓ cups whole wheat flour
    1 ⅓ cups all-purpose flour
    ¼ cup vegetable oil
    1 tsp. baking soda
    ½ tsp. salt

Add only enough to make stiff dough:
    ¾ to 1 cup buttermilk

Knead dough for 30 seconds on a well-floured tabletop. Roll ¼ cup of dough into a ball. Flatten into a circle. Roll dough with a rolling pin to make a 10-inch circle. Place the flatbread on an ungreased cookie sheet. Bake at 350° for about 10 minutes. Bread is done when it is crisp and browned around the edges. Repeat the process with the remaining dough. Break circles into smaller pieces. Serve plain or with butter or cheese.

CULTURAL CONNECTIONS

CONNECT 1: Locate international cookbooks from other Scandinavian countries. (U.S. cookbooks may have sections featuring foreign foods.) Give students time to compare Norwegian foods and menus with Danish, Swedish, and Finnish. Are there more similarities or differences? Ask them to share their findings in a creative way.

CONNECT 2: From the foods mentioned in the preceding article, have a small committee of students create a smorgasbord for a family celebration. They should write the items they will include in the Scandinavian buffet and then create a grocery list that will include the ingredients needed to produce the dishes they have selected.

CONNECT 3: Create a student activity sheet from the Norwegian foods below. Put the Norwegian words in one column, the translations in another, and see if students can match them.

beets = rodbete
carrots = gulroter
cucumber = agurk
peas = erter
tomato = tomat

Brussel sprouts = rosenkal
cauliflower = blomkal
onion = lauk
radish = reddik
spinach = spinat

apple = eple
cherry = kirsebaer
peach = fersken
raisin = rosin
lemon = sutrib
strawberries = hirdbaer

banana = banan
orange = applesin
pineapple = ananas
raspberries = bringebaer
grapes = druer
rhubarb = rabarbra

In 1000 B.C., iron tools came into use on the sub-continent of India and agriculture advanced more quickly than it had in years prior to that time. As more land became necessary for crops, forests were cleared. Irrigation systems were developed so drier parts of the nation could be used for farming.

Rice and wheat have been major food crops in India for centuries. Groundnuts (for oil) and mung beans are two less familiar products under cultivation by Indian farmers. Efforts to increase food production for India's large population include training programs, satellite studies, increased use of chemicals to ensure higher yields, development of better seeds, and improved irrigation practices.

Rice and wheat remain staple crops for the Indian diet. Fish, meat, vegetables, and lentils are also eaten regularly. Yogurt, milk, curd (like cottage cheese), and *ghee* (clarified butter) are also found on Indian tables. *Chapati*, a bread that resembles a pancake, is one of several kinds of bread eaten here.

Curry is well-known in Indian recipes. The combination of herbs, seasonings, and spices can produce peppery hot dishes but others are mild and tasty. One hundred different types of spices are used in the preparation of Indian dishes. Turmeric is one of the most common spices used in curry. Commercial curry powder is readily available and convenient to use.

Indian families might prepare the following for a typical meal:

meat or fish curry	pickles or chutney
assorted vegetables	bread
rice or lentils	fruit for dessert

Religious and regional differences are seen in Indian cooking. In some areas pork and beef are not eaten. Muslims do not eat pork. Hindus avoid beef. Chicken and lamb are the most popular and widely used meats.

For the most part, dishes prepared by Indians in the south are spicier than those in other parts of the country. Northern dishes are milder and sweeter than foods in the south. The *tandoori*, a clay oven, was first used in the north of India but is popular throughout the nation today.

Try this Indian Dish:

Mushroom Curry

Heat in a pan:
    1 Tbs. oil or ghee

Fry in pan until soft:
    1 onion, chopped,
    1 tsp. minced ginger root

Add:
    ½ lb. whole button mushrooms
    1 tomato, chopped

⅓ cup water
1 tsp. salt
½ tsp. chili powder
¼ tsp. turmeric

Cover and cook slowly for 5 minutes. Before serving sprinkle with 2 Tbs. chopped coriander leaves.

CULTURAL CONNECTIONS

CONNECT 1: Familiarize the class with these Indian products that are less common in our country... chick peas, soy beans, mung beans, ground nuts, green and yellow lentils, baisen flour (which comes from ground, split, black chick peas). Have students draw pictures or find actual samples to place on a chart to be displayed in the room. While they are investigating, they may find other examples to include on the chart.

CONNECT 2: The British were responsible for introducing tea to India from China. Have each student design a small handbook with cutouts or drawings that could inform any reader of the procedures for cultivating, harvesting, and processing tea.

CONNECT 3: Recall the role that spices played in the early explorations of the Europeans. Ask for a group of volunteers to assemble a display of common and uncommon spices. Small plastic bags could be used to hold the spices. Have students add labels and attach them to a posterboard for easy display. Encourage them to try to include Indian spices such as cardamom, cumin, coriander, chili, cloves, cinnamon, and fenugreek (the seed of a clover-like Eurasian plant). Let the rest of the class members smell and taste the collection samples.

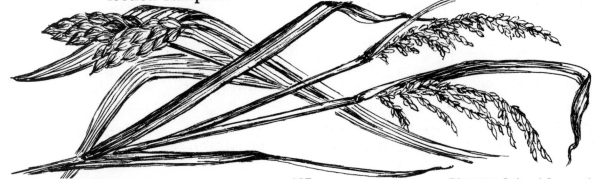

Russians use a traditional word for welcoming guests. From the old custom of offering bread *(khelb)* and salt *(sol)* to people who come visiting evolved the word *khlebosol stro.* Russians have always liked to eat in the company of family and friends.

Foods for the tables of the people in the cold, northern areas of the former Soviet Union come from the southern and central regions where crops are grown more easily. In small villages and in large cities, residents are urged to plant gardens to grow fruit and vegetables for their own use. Where possible, animals are also raised for food.

Refrigeration is not all that common among Russians. So, of necessity, residents shop daily at the supermarkets or in small open-air marketplaces. Supplies are less reliable in the supermarkets but prices are often higher in the marketplaces. Potatoes, vegetables, beef, pork, breads, and dairy products are found most often.

A simple Russian meal might include a thick soup or stew with bread and pickles. On more elaborate occasions an appetizer such as caviar would be followed with meat or fish and salad. Beverages and Russian cakes for dessert would complete the meal.

With over 100 ethnic groups across this largest nation in the world, it is not surprising to find a wide range of tastes and cooking styles. Geography and climate are also major factors in determining how Russians cook and eat. Red meat, root crops, and rye bread are common in the north. Dairy products are most plentiful in the western Baltic republics. In the south the influence of the Mid East is "tasted" in spices and herbs for fish, meat, and fresh vegetables served there.

Try this Russian recipe:

Borscht (Beet Soup)

1. Place a 1-lb. beef shinbone in 8 cups of water. Bring to a boil and simmer for 20 minutes to make meat stock.

2. To the stock add:
   1 eight-ounce can of beets, grated
   2 medium potatoes, peeled and chopped
   1 carrot, peeled and grated
   1 bay leaf
   1 tsp. salt
   ½ tsp. pepper

3. Cook those six ingredients in the stock for 10 minutes. Then add:

   ½ head cabbage, shredded
   1 large onion, thinly sliced
   2 large tomatoes, chopped
   1 tsp. sugar
   2 Tbs. vinegar

4. Cook 30 minutes more. Then remove and leave to cool.

5. Remove meat from the bone. Place deboned meat into the soup. Reheat to boiling. Serve with a generous spoonful of sour cream and a thick slice of fresh, hot bread.

CULTURAL CONNECTIONS

CONNECT 1: Ask each student to draw or use magazine cutouts to produce a place setting for a Russian meal, and label the items with these words featuring Russian pronunciations:

knife = nohsh
fork = VEEL-koo
salt = sohl

spoon = LOHSH-koo
napkin = sahl-FYEHT-koo
pepper = PYEH-reets

CONNECT 2: To emphasize the variance in ethnic groups found in Russia, give students copies of an outline map and have them place names of various groups in the general areas in which they live. Reference books in your library will have listings of the peoples they need. When they have finished, ask them to imagine and discuss the number of different diets, holiday foods, and methods of preparation. Multiplying all these by the number of ethnic groups produces an infinite variety in eating habits. Students will enjoy discussing the possibilities.

CONNECT 3: Ask small groups of students to create word puzzles (crosswords, acrostics, or seek-and-finds) using food-related words.

CONNECT 4: Have them design and produce clever grocery ads such as those that appear in papers in the United States. They should create this one as it might appear in a Russian paper, selecting typical foods that would be available during the peak growing season. They may include prices if they wish.

The food eaten by the Chinese people is simple, nutritious, delicious, and economical. The people make good use of all food products grown in this large Asian nation.

Farming has always been China's chief occupation. Despite China's large population, only 13 percent of its land is suitable for cultivation. Because fresh supplies were not always available to Chinese cooks, chopping food into small pieces became a common practice. Chopping food and cooking it quickly enabled the preparer to retain flavor and vitamin content. Noodles and rice provided filler for the meal. Vegetables, which were more common, were added to increase serving sizes. If possible, meat, fish, or poultry was also included.

The Chinese are sociable eaters, enjoying meals with family and friends. Chopsticks are still used for eating the main dish. Spoons are provided for soups and desserts.

Rice has been cultivated in China for over 5,000 years. It is usually boiled or steamed to be included with meat or vegetable stir fry. Rice may also be pounded into flour for dumplings, noodles, and pastries. It is also used to make wine.

Soybeans are a reliable, versatile, and nutritious crop that grows well in China. They are an important ingredient in Chinese cuisine. Bean sprouts, soy sauce (made from fermented soybeans and wheat), soy flour, tofu (bean curd), soycakes to serve with syrup, and roasted soy nuts are some of the ways the protein-rich soybean is prepared. Other important grains for the Chinese include wheat, millet, and barley.

Chinese food varies by region. Cantonese-style dishes are light and delicate. This is most often the style of Chinese cuisine served in the United States. Szechwan food is hot and spicy with liberal uses of onions, garlic, and hot peppers. Shanghai style features the seafoods that are readily available on the eastern coast. Mongolian food is heavier with more meat and is often barbecued. Mandarin or Peking/Beijing cooking features wheat more than rice as a main ingredient. This area is also famous for the Peking duck.

Try this Chinese dish:

Vegetable Stir Fry

In a large pan or wok, fry in 3 Tbs. oil for ½ minute:
- 1 tsp. garlic
- 1 thinly sliced onion

Add and cook for 1 minute:
- ½ cup finely cut bamboo shoots
- ½ of a red pepper finely cut
- 1 carrot finely cut
- 1 stalk of celery, chopped
- 1 cup of snow peas

Sprinkle with:
- ½ tsp. sugar
- ¼ tsp. salt
- 1 Tbs. soy sauce

Serve your vegetable stir-fry while it is hot.

CULTURAL CONNECTIONS

CONNECT 1: Have students write variations of this recipe, adapting it to fit their tastes or to include vegetables most available in their area. Encourage them to consider texture and color as they write the recipes. If it is possible, prepare two or three of the student recipes in the classroom so that everyone can have a taste. Suggest that all the students prepare their recipes at home to share with their families.

CONNECT 2: Create a Chinese restaurant in your classroom. Browse through other Chinese cookbooks available through a public library or from individuals in your neighborhood. Let your students select some dishes that sound appealing and design a menu for use in their own restaurant. Some students can make a colorful, attractive cover. Others can list the dishes that are available and assign prices to them.

CONNECT 3: Have class members research authentic holidays and festivals that are celebrated in China today and find special dishes or treats that are prepared as part of each celebration. As a class project, students can make a small recipe booklet of festival foods and include drawings. Cooks enjoy seeing how a recipe will look when it is done.

GERMAN FOOD

The foods of Germany reflect the variety of cultural influences in this European nation. Eating habits also reflect geographical and historical differences.

In northern Germany where land touches sea, fish dishes are common. The northern plains are crop growing areas. Wheat, barley, oats, and potatoes are common there. Where Germany borders the Netherlands, animals graze on the lush pasture grasses. Beef and lamb are important dietary features there. Hogs and potatoes have always been raised and consumed by Germans.

Germany is the fourth largest producer of meat and dairy products in the world but must import fruit and vegetables from sunnier places in southern Europe. The nation is a leader among nations in the export of beer.

German sausage (*wurst*) has a world-wide reputation. Two hundred kinds of breads and cheeses have become common companions to bockwurst, leberwurst, bierwurst, bratwurst, frankfurters, and other meats. Common dishes that might accompany the meats include sauerkraut and dumplings. Pretzels are a favorite German snack food.

German meals are:

Fruhstuck - Breakfast foods are bread, cheese, sausage, honey, and jam. Adults drink coffee or tea while milk or hot chocolate are popular breakfast beverages for children. Since World War II, cereals, fruit juices, and yogurt have become popular, also.

Mittsagessen - Midday meals are apt to be soups with meat, egg casseroles, and boiled potatoes. Rice pudding or fruit compotes are common desserts.

Abendbrot - Evening meals might include breads with cold meat and cheese, salad, and pickles.

Holidays are special days calling for special recipes and dishes. Cakes, pastries, cookies, and tarts are favorites among adults and children.

Try this German recipe:

Potato Pancakes (KARTOFFELPUFFER)

Peel, then grate, 2 pounds of potatoes

Finely chop 1 onion

Mix potatoes and onion with 2 beaten eggs, 1 tsp. salt

Prepare a frying pan with no-stick cooking spray. When pan is hot, drop in spoonfuls of potato mixture. Press flat. Cook until golden and crisp, about three minutes on each side. Serve immediately with applesauce as a side dish.

CULTURAL CONNECTIONS

CONNECT 1: Help students make and serve the Kartoffelpuffer mentioned here. How do they compare with potato dishes with which class members are familiar?

CONNECT 2: Start a collection of potato recipes. Perhaps each member of the class could contribute a family favorite for a class potato book. The recipe book might be created in the shape of a large potato with a brown cover.

CONNECT 3: Assign students to try to locate someone in the community or neighborhood who is of German heritage and interview him or her on a subject or subjects of interest to them. If possible, invite several of these people to the class to speak about unique features of German ancestry.

CONNECT 4: Divide students into small groups and have each group create a learning device (chart, flash cards, pictures) to teach others about these foods in German...
cheese - der Kase
potatoes - die Kartoffeln
egg - das Ei
salad - der Salat
fruit - das Fruit
meat - das Fleisch
bread - das Brot
roll - das Brotchen
sausage - die Wurst
cake - der Kuchen
pastry - die Torte

If students wish to do some research, the groups can include some additional foods.

FRENCH FOOD

The French have two styles of cooking, the simple home cooking and *haute* (oht) or grand cuisine. The latter originated among chefs who worked for the kings and queens of years past. These meals were complicated and required hours and many special ingredients to prepare them. The French nobility no longer exists, but haute cuisine is practiced today by famous chefs.

One of the biggest effects on the cooking of France has been geography. In Normandy on the northeast coast, orchards thrive and cattle graze on the grasses beneath the trees. In Brittany, a less productive area southwest of Normandy, people have relied upon the sea rather than on the land as a major food source. In Provence in extreme southwest France, near Italy, the diet resembles that of the Italians. In the Pyrenees in the south, French and Spanish cooking blend.

Breakfasts in France vary with the seasons. Hearty, filling meals for cold times might include potatoes, eggs, bacon, and hot cereal. On warmer days, pastry with coffee or hot chocolate are enjoyed. The *croissant* (kwah SAHN) and crisp French bread *(baguette)* are widely known.

Lunch is usually served around noon. Soup is a favorite or an omelet or quiche with salad are commonly served. Dessert is typically cheese and fruit.

Dinner is most often served between 7 p.m. and 8 p.m. If lunch was light, dinner might be a meal with four to five courses. (People who have a large meal at noon eat lightly in the evening.) Special wines are usually part of the French meal. Meal time in France is an important family time. Friends sharing the meal can make the occasion special.

Try this French dish:

Quiche Lorraine

Preheat oven to 350°. In a medium-sized bowl beat with an eggbeater or whisk:
- 4 eggs
- 1 cup whipping cream
- ¼ tsp. salt
- dash of pepper
- ¼ tsp. nutmeg

Pierce with a fork the bottom and sides of a 9" unbaked pie shell

Sprinkle in the bottom of the pie shell:
- 1 to 1½ cups grated Swiss cheese
- ½ lb. browned, crumbled bacon

Pour egg mixture atop cheese and bacon. Bake 45-50 minutes or until browned. Cool a few minutes, then slice. Refrigerate any leftovers.

CULTURAL CONNECTIONS

CONNECT 1: Assign a class project to create an attractively designed and illustrated cooking dictionary. Students should include terms that are needed for successful cookery. Examples might include *mince, sauté, preheat, brown, marinate, knead, garnish, strain, shred, grease,* and *grate.* Students should think of other examples.

CONNECT 2: Ask for a group of volunteers to set up a simple place setting of dishes similar to one in a French restaurant. They should correctly place the dishes, utensils, glasses, and napkin. An etiquette book will offer assistance and perhaps a bit of history on correctly setting a table. Have the group explain their research findings as they demonstrate the correct usage of all the pieces in the place setting.

CONNECT 3: Assign another group of students to prepare a chart containing 8–10 kitchen safety rules and include pictures wherever they would add interest and help to make the work area safe. Suggestions for tips might be use of potholders, cutting on a cutting board, frequent washing of hands, washing fruits and vegetables before cooking, use of soda or salt on cooking fires, and ways to prevent steam burns.

Africa, the world's second largest continent, covers nearly 12 million square miles. The peoples who live here represent many different cultural groups and life styles. Their diets are as varied as the landscapes of their homelands.

Many Africans traditionally eat two meals a day, late morning and late evening. Frequent snacks are enjoyed in such cases, although these are rarely sweet snacks. Those following more Western lifestyles eat three times a day—breakfast, lunch, and dinner. Sadly, people in many parts of Africa do not eat regularly at all.

With limited refrigeration, daily shopping for fresh foods from the local market is common. The variety of fruits and vegetables available is vast. Cabbages, cucumbers, oranges, and bananas can be purchased along with cassavas, star apples, tamarinds, and plantains. Many of these products were introduced to African soil by explorers and settlers. Native food crops include millet, sorghum, and the oil palm. Ninety percent of the plants cultivated around the world can be grown in African soils.

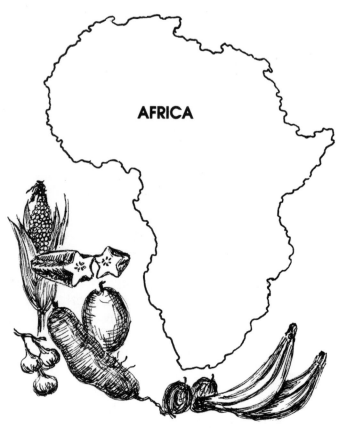

AFRICA

Recipes of Africa are easily adaptable to ingredients at hand. Meat, fish, and poultry are in limited supply. Thick soups and stews with fresh vegetables are nutritious despite the fact that they lack great quantities of proteins. The starch for the African diet can be found in the forms of rice, bread, or *fufu*.

An interesting tradition from the past among East and West African cooks is that recipes were never written down. They were passed from family to family by word of mouth.

Try this African dish:

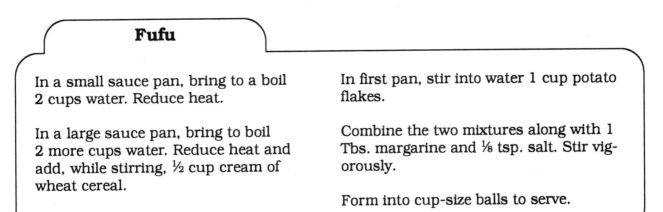

Fufu

In a small sauce pan, bring to a boil 2 cups water. Reduce heat.

In a large sauce pan, bring to boil 2 more cups water. Reduce heat and add, while stirring, ½ cup cream of wheat cereal.

In first pan, stir into water 1 cup potato flakes.

Combine the two mixtures along with 1 Tbs. margarine and ⅛ tsp. salt. Stir vigorously.

Form into cup-size balls to serve.

CULTURAL CONNECTIONS

CONNECT 1: Divide the class into five groups to do some research to learn more about the African plantain. Group one will report to the class on how it grows, group two on how it is harvested, group three on ways it can be prepared and eaten, group four on the plant family to which it belongs. Group five can draw and color other unusual members of its family.

CONNECT 2: Studying foods from many parts of the world, we begin to notice many similarities. Point out that African chapatties are very similar to Mexican tortillas. Encourage class members to learn more about both and share the results on a Venn diagram.

CONNECT 3: Many African grains are prepared for cooking with a mortar and pestle. Have groups of students draw pictures or create models with which they can demonstrate how this ancient apparatus helps change grains to other products.

CONNECT 4: Cooks in Nigeria often make soup flavored with *egusi seeds*. See what information students can locate about this product. How does it grow? How is it harvested? What do we use regularly that is similar?

Barley

Easily adapted to varied climates. Used for animals and as beverage malt.

Research the origin of barleycorn and John Barleycorn.

Corn

Only important cereal of American origin.

Interview a person who knows corn breeding. Ask for an explanation of how hybrid seed is produced. Prepare a poster to show the process.

Cassava

Also known as yucca and manioc. Source of tapioca.

Draw and color the plant and fruit of the cassava. Prepare tapioca (from a mix available at the grocery store) to serve the class.

Millet

A staple of the world's poorest people.

Show a family tree of grains that illustrates that millet and sorghum are sisters.

This activity page describes the WORLD'S MAJOR FOODS. Pick and choose activities to be part of a contract. Or work out a plan for a cooperative-learning group to do all of the activities.

Every year, peoples of the world devour over 1.2 billion metric tons of cereal grains. Those who live in poorer nations eat the cereals directly, consuming 400 pounds a year per person. In developed countries, cereal grains are converted and eaten in the form of dairy products, eggs, and meat.

Oats

Rich in protein and carbohydrates. A favorite of breakfast eaters.

Draw and label the seed head and a cross-section of the oat grain including the bran, endosperm and embryo or germ.

Potato

World's most important vegetable. Native to the Andes.

Write a story about a family in Ireland who survived the Irish potato famine of the 1840s.

Rice

One person in three depends on rice for survival.

Investigate the unusual growing conditions for rice. Sketch the small machines used to plant and harvest this crop.

Rye

Crossed with wheat, it makes *triticale*, richer than either parent.

Show the steps in the production of triticale.

Sorghum

An African grass, most versatile.

Molasses to broom straw, including food for animals and humans. Write an article that might be published in a magazine informing people about this versatile grass.

Soybean

U.S. farmers plant one acre in six to soybeans.

Draw the myriad of products from hamburger extender to an ingredient in linoleum that come from soybeans.

Sweet Potato

Belongs to the morning glory family.

Write a time line of events that shows the work George Washington Carver did with the potato and other food products.

Wheat

Monarch of the cereal grains.

Grow some wheat in the classroom. Keep a pictorial record of its major growth stages.

Name: _____

SHOPPING TRIP

Family meals from around the world call for different recipes and different ingredients. Choose a location in which you are interested. Picture the setting for a food shopping trip. Draw the setting. Decide on the characters. Include conversation.

Decide whether you would like this picture series to be serious or humorous. In either case, portray realities. Your finished product should resemble a page from a comic book.

1.

2.

3.

4.

5.

6.

7.

MATH AND MUFFINS

Below you will find another recipe, this one using one of the world's major grains as a main ingredient. Make and bake these wheat muffins if you would like. But here, use the recipe for a math lesson with fractions.

In the designated boxes, increase the main recipe so that it is doubled. In the other space, cut the recipe in half, for a smaller amount.

Wheat Muffins

3 cups whole wheat flour
⅔ cup brown sugar
1 tsp. salt
4½ tsps. baking powder
1⅓ cup milk
2 eggs, beaten
⅓ cup safflower, corn, or soy oil
¼ cup honey

1. Preheat the oven to 375°.

2. Sift all dry ingredients together.

3. Combine eggs, milk, shortening and honey in a second bowl.

4. Combine the two mixtures until just moistened.

5. Fill baking cups ⅔ full. Bake for 20 minutes.

Makes 18 muffins.

Ingredients Doubled

Recipe Cut in Half

THE WHOLE MILK STORY

In the history of man, the domestication of animals for use in work and as food was an important chapter. When or how the idea of using the milk of animals as a food began is uncertain. We do know that milk is a nutritious, recommended part of our diets.

There are many types of animals that produce milk for peoples of the world.

Unscramble the words in the paragraphs below to get the whole story.

The *zebu*, in the nation of (ndaiI) _____, does not give as much milk as the dairy cow. The (eubz) _____ is also called a (hmrBaan) _____, a sacred cow of the subcontinent.

Lapp people who live above the Arctic circle milk (eeerrdni) _____. These animals are also taught to pull a *pulka*, or (dsle) _____. (direnere) _____ milk is rich and (ssteat) _____ very good. The milk is churned to make (scee-he) _____.

In the high (nmnstuiao) _____ of Asia, people raise the *yak* for milk. It has long, thick (rhia) _____. The Chinese call the yak *mow niu*, which means hair (lcetat) _____. It cannot moo. Rather it (nurtsg) _____ like a pig. Yak (kmli) _____ is rich and deep (lodg) _____ in color. It is used to make (utrebt) _____ for the Tibetans.

In hot countries of Asia and Africa, the water (auflobf) _____ provides (ilkm) _____. This animal is strong and is also used for (rkwo) _____. It is so (neetlg) _____, a child can manage it. To ensure a good milk supply, the (bfafuol) _____ must cool off in (awter) _____ once a day.

The (tgoa) _____ is called the "poor man's cow." It is milked today on the continents of (aAis) _____, (cfiAar) _____, (mrAicae) _____ and (pruEeo) _____. The female must be milked (ereht) _____ times a day to keep the supply flowing. She may give (limk) _____ enough to equal (net) _____ times her weight in a (ryae) _____.

CHAPTER 7
CURRENCY

Analyzing and comparing the currency and coins of various cultures can reveal art, mythology, hairstyles, dress, even religion. Each cultural group has its own money system. The features found on coins have actually changed little over the years.

Any money system or currency can be used for these purposes:
   1) for use as a medium of exchange (something others will accept in trade)
   2) as a store of wealth (something to save for later use)
   3) as an account unit (something with which to buy goods or pay for services)

Barter systems were used prior to official money systems. Animals, animal hides, gold and silver, salt, even cloth were among early bartering items. Other unusual items used around the world include beads made of shells called *wampum* and bean-shaped lumps of silver and gold called *electrum*. It took several hundred years for these systems to be replaced with coins as a medium of exchange.

The first coins were made around 600 B.C. in western Turkey. Other ancient coins have been found by archeologists in China and India. In early Greece those men who made coins were considered skilled artists. The Romans made coins in their temple which honored Juno or Moneta. It is from this that we get our word *money*. The soldiers of the Roman Empire were often paid in salt. Salt money was called *salarium*. It is from this that we get our word *salary*.

Marco Polo noted the use of paper money among the Chinese. In his account of his travels in the Orient he wrote of bark paper money used by the Chinese people.

Numisma in Latin and *nomisma* in Greek both mean "coin." It is from these languages that we get *numismatics* and *numismatists*—coin collecting and coin collectors.

To know a culture's exchange system is to know its uniqueness, its history, and the currency it uses for exchange of goods and services.

CULTURAL CONNECTIONS

CONNECT 1: Give students some modeling clay to use in sculpting reproductions of coins of particular interest to them. Both sides can be carved into a single coin-shaped lump of clay or for easier display, students can create one-sided coins and create the likenesses so both sides can be displayed at the same time.

Use plaster of paris for longer-lasting models of coins.

Bank notes can be reproduced with paper and colored pencils.

CONNECT 2: Contact a representative at a local bank to assist the class with tracking a designated currency. Keep a daily log of any fluctuation in the value of the selected nation's monetary unit.

CONNECT 3: Let students produce rubbings from actual coins available from other students in the room or from collectors in the community who would be willing to share coins with the class.

CONNECT 4: Have each student select a symbol from coins or currency. Examples might include famous people, buildings, animals, or mythological characters. Then he/she can enlarge the selected picture on paper with an ink or colored drawing.

CONNECT 5: Ask local numismatists to come to the classroom to share, show, and tell about their collections.

CONNECT 6: Compare and contrast present-day United States' coins with collectables from foreign lands. Class members can create varied displays based on coins' sizes, designs, values, weights, and materials from which they are made. Brainstorm other categories of comparison.

CONNECT 7: Students can design paper money and coins representative of them and their families. Whose pictures could be used? What symbols and designs would be appropriate? Will they use one- or two-sided coins? Encourage them to invent clever names for their own personal currency systems.

CONNECT 8: Have student groups create puzzles, games, and flashcards to help others learn the names of coins and bank notes for nations they study.

CONNECT 9: For a class project, have students create a kit of materials that could be used for coin collecting. They should write hints on how to care for coins, what to do, and what not to do to preserve valuable samples, how to display the collection, equipment and tools to use, and possible themes upon which to base the collection.

CONNECT 10: Secure a copy of Joe Cribb's book, *Money*, from *The Eyewitness Series*, 1990, Alfred A. Knopf Co., New York. It is an excellent pictorial reference source for classroom use.

AFRICAN CURRENCY

In tribal societies such as those found in Africa, cultures have had objects recognized by all as valuable. These objects, which do not resemble typical coins or bank notes, were counted out and used as payment for goods.

Iron hoes were used as wedding payments, lengths of cloth had trading value, copper rings known as *manillas* were used among the Ibo peoples of Nigeria. Bars of rock salt bound with reeds to prevent breaking were used in Ethiopia. In eastern Africa cattle were and still are regarded as symbols of wealth.

The Greeks were the first peoples to issue coins in Africa. Their coins were introduced in Libya on the Mediterranean Sea. They were followed by monies brought to Africa by Phoenicians, Romans, and Byzantines. Local African groups also produced coins for use in buying and selling goods.

The camel caravans of the Arabs and the Berbers moving across the Sahara helped carry gold from West Africa to European and Mideastern mints. When outsiders formed colonies on the continent, they brought their own forms of money and these were used in addition to traditional currencies.

Some unusual forms of payment found in Africa include
    –gold rings from Sudan
    –stamp money used in Madagascar
    –iron wire flattened at both ends used by the Kissi people of Liberia

Pictured on traditional coin shapes seen today are African wildlife, national heroes, important events in history, crops and plants, and geometric designs.

Historical connections can often be seen in the present-day notes and coins of African nations. These countries have monetary systems based on 100 cents:
    Kenya's *shilling*   Zimbabwe's *dollar*
    Ethiopia's *birr*   South Africa's *rand*

Other systems are:
    Botswana's *pula* based on 100 thebes
    Zambia's *kwacha* based on 100 ngwee
    Nigeria's *naira* based on 100 kobo
    Egypt's *pound* based on 100 piasters
    Algeria's *dinar* based on 100 centimes
    Morocco's *dirham* based on 100 centimes

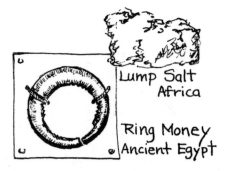

Lump Salt Africa

Ring Money Ancient Egypt

INDIAN CURRENCY

Coins and bank notes in India, as in other parts of the world, are symbols of financial status and a means to pay for goods and services. But they are also evidence of the country's nationhood. Printed and engraved currency depicts national leaders, historical events, cultural achievement, and social ideals.

India's basic unit is the *rupee*, divided into 100 *pice* (rhymes with rice). It is printed in denominations of 1, 5, 10, 20, 50, and 100.

Because of the variety in India's languages, the phrase "one (or other denomination) rupee" appears in 13 different tongues on the bank note. The paper notes are different sizes and are printed in different colors of ink. Coins also vary in size. This is helpful as an aid to the large numbers of people who cannot read.

On Indian paper money, you can also see a blank space next to the face of the note. This is the space for the watermark. Held to the light, the Ashokan lion can be seen in this space. This is an aid in the prevention of counterfeiting. The Ashokan lion became the governmental symbol after India gained its independence from Britain in 1947. The animal can also be seen on Indian coins.

Another common symbol found on Indian monetary units is the *chakra* or wheel. The chakra is also seen on the flag of India. Shafts of wheat are another image often found on Indian coins. Pictures seen on the back of bank notes include samples of architecture and scenes depicting progress in agriculture, sea trade, and hydroelectric power.

Compared to U.S. coins, the Indian monetary system has added denominations. Indians use 1-pice, 2-pice, 5-pice, 10-pice, 25-pice (the quarter rupee), and 50-pice coins.

The currency monetary unit in Germany is the *Mark* which is divided into 100 *Pfennings.* The *Pfennia* was the name of a silver coin used as long ago as the eleventh century.

In the early history of Germany and its neighbors, Austria, Switzerland, Poland, and Czechoslovakia, each kingdom, city, and state had its own monetary system. Some of the currencies used were *guilder, ducats,* and *thalers.*

Thalers of the 1500s and 1600s were highly decorative, creative miniatures of art as well as mediums of exchange. *Thaler* was short for Joachimsthaler, which came from the Joachimsthal mine, a large silver mine in Bohemia, and is the base for the English word *dollar.*

Early drawings and engravings depict fourteenth and fifteenth century coin-makers at work. These views of process plus samples of actual coins make this page of history quite complete.

Early German coins were made of gold and silver, some with a flat, plain edge set apart from the center design by a ridge.

Iron coins came into being at the time of World War I. As the war continued, the mark became less and less valuable. One paper note in Cologne was issued with eight zeroes. People had difficulty dealing with all the zeroes that appeared on the notes. Following World War I, this paper money became all but worthless and it was used as wallpaper. Children used tied bundles of the worthless money as building blocks.

With the fall of the Berlin Wall and the reunification of Germany, the mark has undergone another historical change. The conversion from the German Democratic Republic marks to the West German deutsche marks created many problems. The rate of exchange was hotly debated. There were concerns about wages, business investments, savings accounts, and private ownership of East German government industries.

In July of 1990, the West German mark with a 1:1 conversion rate became the new currency of the new nation. Economic union was a must despite the fact that the conversion and adjustment would hurt certain segments of the economy.

The earliest evidence of peoples who made coins of one sort or another in Great Britain is seen in findings from the Celts, Romans, Anglo-Saxons, and the Vikings. All these groups made contributions to the lineage of British coins.

In most areas of the British Isles, the monetary system today is the *pound sterling* which is divided into 100 pennies. The sterling coin dates back to Edward I, who in 1279 made a new penny of silver. Robert the Bruce, King of Scotland, followed Edward's example, but had his likeness in the center of his coin shown in profile, unlike Edward's front view.

The Elizabeth I silver sixpence was the first coin to be made with the new screw press device. With this new method of production, Britain had machine-produced money.

Pound coins of gold evolved through the years. Elaborate designs of kings on thrones, heads of kings, and crests and coats of arms appeared on coins struck in the Royal Mint near the Tower of London.

In the eighteenth century paper notes became popular. The Scottish guinea note was the first one to be printed in three colors–black, red, and blue.

Some unusual coins that have appeared through time in the British Isles include:
- –a copper half penny
- –a heart-shaped half penny
- –brass farthings (quarter pennies)
- –cartwheels, thick-rimmed steam press coins
- –a Welsh druid half penny made of copper

As Vikings traveled to England, Germany, and France they confiscated and traded goods. Coins from Europe and the Islamic lands came into the Vikings' possession. By the tenth or eleventh century kings of Scandinavia began to make their own coins. These monetary units were silver, irregularly round, and were often decorated with the king's likeness. Other early monies were Scandinavian reproductions of Islamic coins with circular border designs surrounding a center symbol. The kings often invited English coinmakers to their lands to mint coins.

Silver coins from the thirteenth century have been found with simple marks on just one side. By the sixteenth and seventeenth centuries, Danish kings were issuing square coins. Known as *klippe*, they were easier to mint than round coins and were used in a war emergency. Coins of this era had become quite decorative and sophisticated. The basic design remained, a border, often with letters and geometric markings, with the king's likeness or decorative symbol in the center.

Plate coins made of copper from Falun in Sweden were the largest coins ever made. They were rectangular and the largest ones weighed over 40 pounds! Easier-to-handle paper money was soon introduced in Sweden, the first European country to issue paper money.

Through the years, *dalers* became common coins. King Gustav issued a silver daler in the 1500s. Paper dalers could be seen in the 1700s. And the Swedish copper dalers that appeared following a war with Russia were decorated with the Roman gods—Jupiter, Mars, Mercury, and Saturn.

Lapp people in northern Scandinavia relied on the reindeer and other live animals and animal fur as a means of exchange.

Common systems of currency came into Denmark, Norway, and Sweden in the late 1800s. *Kronor* (now referred to as *krona*) meaning "crown" was divided into 100 *ore*. The *ore* had been a Swedish coin. The *krone* or *krona* had been Norwegian and Danish. Coins and currency for Finland changed as those people came under the rule of their neighbors, Sweden, and then Russia. When Finland finally gained its independence in 1917, it kept the Russian system of *markha* and *penni* and it is still in use there today. Some Finnish bank notes use Finnish, Swedish, and Russian languages on them.

Among the early coins of Belgium and The Netherlands is a Celtic gold sample by the Nervii people decorated with a primitively designed horse. Later from the eleventh century through the sixteenth century, the Dukes of Burgundy were responsible for the most issues of gold and silver coins. Competing with them were nobles, villages, and even religious leaders who had the authority to create their own monetary symbols.

In the 1200s these Low Countries were centers of trade from around the world. Numerous foreign currencies were common in Antwerp, Amsterdam, and other commercial port cities.

As the Dutch peoples revolted against their Spanish ruler in the late 1500s, *seige money* was often issued by cities involved in the fighting. One very unusual example was a coin of cardboard made in Leiden in 1574.

The Dutch empire of the 1600s possessed colonies that provided trade opportunities in many parts of the world. In Ceylon a bar of copper came into use as a coin. The Dutch *daalder*, patterned after the Spanish pieces of eight, was put into use in the Far East.

Today, The Netherlands uses *gilden* currency based on a 100-cent decimal system. Belgium adopted the French system of *francs*. Because Belgium has two official languages, French and Flemish, it has issued coins with both languages on them and more recently two separate sets of coins. It is also interesting that paper money in Belgium today has raised dots to assist the visually impaired.

The Greeks introduced coins to peoples on the Iberian peninsula. The Greeks' mint was located in the vicinity of Ampurias in northeast Spain.

These early coins were irregularly round, silver, and had simple center designs of people and animals. Small, scored borders were often used to add just a touch of decoration to the outer edges.

Roman and Carthaginian inhabitants in Spain made coins of copper and silver bearing the images of animals and fish.

The gold coins of the Moors displayed Islamic designs of geometric shapes with language inscriptions around their circumferences.

The voyages of Columbus and Vasco da Gama opened up new sources for silver and gold to be used for coinage. Portugal's colonies in the area of Malaya were convenient sources of tin for money issued locally.

The Spanish form of money today is the *peseta*. Introduced in 1869, this term is used for both paper money and coins.

The Portuguese currently use the *escudo* based on 100 *centavos*. This system first appeared in 1915.

ORIENTAL CURRENCY

As early as 500 B.C., the Chinese created coins from bronze; these coins were cast in the shapes of tools such as knives and hoes, but were too fragile for actual use. Cowrie shell-shaped money was also common. The shells themselves were used as payment 3,500 years ago in China. When the Chinese developed their system of writing, the shape of the shell became the symbol for money.

China's first emperor, Qin Shi Huangdi, replaced the tool shapes with round coins with square holes in the centers.

In the first century A.D., the Tang dynasty standardized the coin of Qin Shi Huangdi by adding inscriptions of four characters on each side of the center square. The open middle was used to string coins on a piece of leather or cloth for safe keeping.

The largest bank note ever issued was done so by the Chinese. The hefty piece was 9" x 13" and weighed eight pounds. Not too long after this unwieldy system proved to be unacceptable, the Chinese began to print official paper "receipts."

As late as the nineteenth century, bamboo sticks were used as money in Shanghai. This money, too, was lighter in weight than its comparable value in metal coins.

The Japanese fashioned their coins after those of the Chinese. From the Chinese *yuan* (round coin) came the Japanese *yen.* The Chinese cent is *fen,* meaning hundredth part, while the Japanese cent is the *sen.*

A Japanese bronze coin issued by a *shogun* (military dictator) in 1626 is an exact replica of the standard coin of the Tang dynasty of A.D. 621. Later in the 1600s, Ieyasu reorganized the monetary system of Japan. The coins were similar to previously used ingots and were hammered or cast from gold and silver into small rectangular pieces.

At about this same time, the idea of paper money made its way from China to Japan. Many Buddhist temples issued money and the religious institutions acted as banks. Some of the money took the form of bookmarks and was creatively decorated with designs, nature scenes, and script.

The shogun coin was eventually replaced by Meiji emperor, Mutsuhito, who preferred the "dragon dollar." The dragon appeared in the center surrounded by two dotted circles separated by script.

Today's Japanese yen is one of the most important currencies used in international trade and investment.

CHANGING VALUES

Many factors determine the value of a nation's currency on a given day. Call your local bank to secure the latest value for the German Deutsch Mark compared to the U.S. dollar.

Write the value here:_____

Set up a mathematical formula so that you can convert Deutsch Mark values to amounts in our currency. Use your calculator or mental math, if possible. Write the values within the shapes given below.

FORMULA:_____

DEUTSCH MARKS...Notes

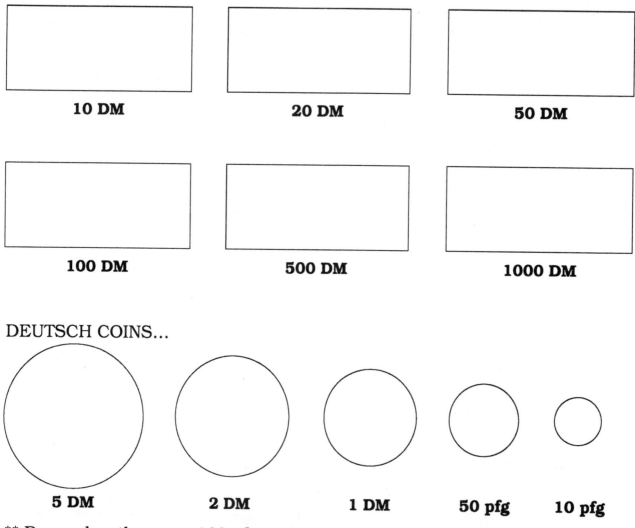

10 DM	**20 DM**	**50 DM**
100 DM	**500 DM**	**1000 DM**

DEUTSCH COINS...

| **5 DM** | **2 DM** | **1 DM** | **50 pfg** | **10 pfg** |

** Remember there are 100 pfennings in one Deutsch Mark.

COMMON LINKS

The first set of words is related to Indian culture.

Think carefully and determine how the second word is related to the first. It could be something as simple as common letters, number of letters, or similar use. Or, it might be more complicated as when both might represent an idea or ideal. There are no *right* answers, but there are *several* common links.

If the class has been divided into groups for this activity, ask the recorder in your group to jot down as many links as he/she can. Perhaps you could challenge another group and see who can produce the longest quality list of links.

Indian Term	Second Word	Common Links
1. Rupee	Dollar	_____
2. Watermark	America's Great Seal	_____
3. Pice	Penny	_____
4. Chakra	Unicycle	_____
5. Ghats	Indus	_____
6. Sari	Kimono	_____
7. Ashokan lion	American eagle	_____
8. New Delhi	The Hague	_____
9. Caste system	One-room school	_____
10. Cobra	Clarinet	_____

CURRENCY HONORS

King Christian IV and King Gustav VI of Sweden were two of the
Scandinavian rulers who had their images placed on coins of their realms.
Other European royalty who were honored in the same way include

Philip of Macedonia - Greece
William of Orange - Holland
Frederick the Great - Prussia
Napoleon Bonaparte - France
Queen Elizabeth - Britain

Who are well-known people from the United States who received the same
honor? Search old and new coins to find the images of these people.
Arrange these people beginning with the person who has lived most recently
(some will no longer be alive, of course). Add names in descending order
until the list is filled. Add a phrase telling about the lifetime accomplishments of each of these people.

APPEARING ON COIN/NOTE   **WHY THEY WERE SO HONORED**

1._____   _____

2._____   _____

3._____   _____

4._____   _____

5._____   _____

6._____   _____

7._____   _____

8._____   _____

9._____   _____

10._____   _____

Who else do you think should be on a coin? _____

AFRICAN CURRENCIES

Here are some of the currencies used on the continent of Africa: centimes, pound, piasters, kwacha, kobo, birr, dollar, dinar, shilling, pula, thebes, ngwee, rand, naira. These names have been started in the puzzle below. Now it is up to you to finish them.

ANSWER KEY

Hidden Treasure   **Page 22**
      Sports stadiums today are based on the
design of the Colosseum.

What/Who Am I?   **Page 25**
      a pagoda
      a pyramid
      Great Wall of China
      the Parthenon

Vases, Vessels, Jugs, and Jars   **Page 52**

```
      H  Y  D  R  I  A    A
                          V
                     L    E   K  y  T  H  O  S
                          S   K  Y  P  H  O  S
A  M  P  H  O  R  A   R    S
      K     R  A  T   A    E        R
            K  Y     L     X
```

Be a Matchmaker   **Page 77**

1. I	7. D
2. L	8. B
3. H	9. E
4. J	10. A
5. C	11. F
6. K	12. G

Danish Diagram   **Page 95**

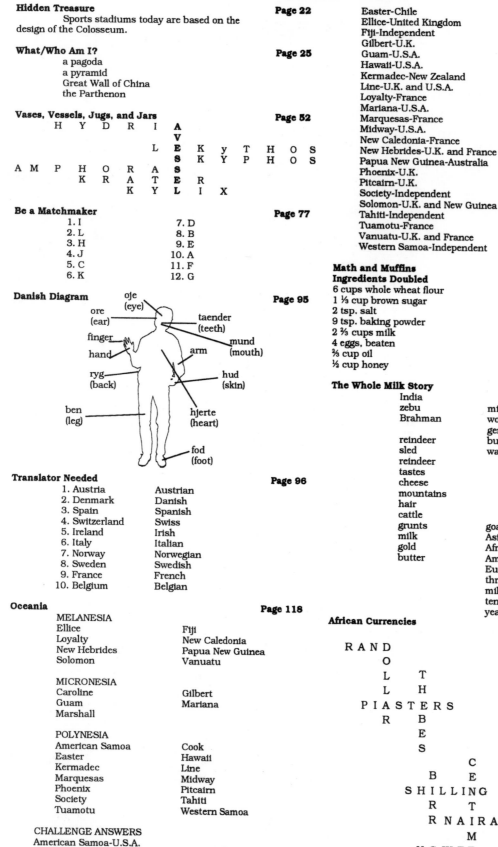

oje (eye)
ore (ear)
taender (teeth)
finger
mund (mouth)
hand
arm
ryg (back)
hud (skin)
ben (leg)
hjerte (heart)
fod (foot)

Translator Needed   **Page 96**

1. Austria	Austrian
2. Denmark	Danish
3. Spain	Spanish
4. Switzerland	Swiss
5. Ireland	Irish
6. Italy	Italian
7. Norway	Norwegian
8. Sweden	Swedish
9. France	French
10. Belgium	Belgian

Oceania   **Page 118**

MELANESIA

Ellice	Fiji
Loyalty	New Caledonia
New Hebrides	Papua New Guinea
Solomon	Vanuatu

MICRONESIA

Caroline	
Guam	Gilbert
Marshall	Mariana

POLYNESIA

American Samoa	Cook
Easter	Hawaii
Kermadec	Line
Marquesas	Midway
Phoenix	Pitcairn
Society	Tahiti
Tuamotu	Western Samoa

CHALLENGE ANSWERS
American Samoa-U.S.A.
Caroline-Independent
Cook-Self governing with help of New Zealand
Easter-Chile
Ellice-United Kingdom
Fiji-Independent
Gilbert-U.K.
Guam-U.S.A.
Hawaii-U.S.A.
Kermadec-New Zealand
Line-U.K. and U.S.A.
Loyalty-France
Mariana-U.S.A.
Marquesas-France
Midway-U.S.A.
New Caledonia-France
New Hebrides-U.K. and France
Papua New Guinea-Australia
Phoenix-U.K.
Pitcairn-U.K.
Society-Independent
Solomon-U.K. and New Guinea
Tahiti-Independent
Tuamotu-France
Vanuatu-U.K. and France
Western Samoa-Independent

Math and Muffins   **Page 140**

Ingredients Doubled	Recipe Cut in Half
6 cups whole wheat flour	1 ½ cups flour
1 ⅓ cup brown sugar	⅓ cup brown sugar
2 tsp. salt	½ tsp. salt
9 tsp. baking powder	2 ¼ tsps. baking powder
2 ⅔ cups milk	⅔ cup milk
4 eggs, beaten	1 egg
⅔ cup oil	⅛ cup oil
½ cup honey	⅛ cup honey

The Whole Milk Story   **Page 141**

India	buffalo
zebu	milk
Brahman	work
	gentle
reindeer	buffalo
sled	water
reindeer	
tastes	
cheese	
mountains	
hair	
cattle	
grunts	goat
milk	Asia
gold	Africa
butter	America
	Europe
	three
	milk
	ten
	year

African Currencies   **Page 155**

```
R A N D                              N
O           T               D I N A R
L           H                         I
L                                     R
P I A S T E R S              P U L A
R           B        K O B O
            E        W       U
            S        A       N
                C    C       D
          B     E    H
     S H I L L I N G A
          R     T
          R N A I R A
                M
     N G W E E
          S
```